KU-078-286

Contents

Chapter One
What Is Britishness?   1

Chapter Two
The Stories We Tell Ourselves   21

Chapter Three
From Armada To Empire   36

Chapter Four
In Love With Shakespeare   57

Chapter Five
Class, Culture And Money   70

Chapter Six
The Great Hero's Chapter   90

Chapter Seven
The Lion And The Unicorn: The British Brand   105

Post-Script
Last Night of the Dogs – August 16th 2008
Walthamstow Stadium   129

End Notes   135

Further Reading   142

UP THE BRITISH

501 469 161

FF 14 9161

The author would like to thank:
Helen, Harriet and my history teacher at Kings Norton Grammar
School
for Boys. Birmingham 1968-70. (Mr Davies?)

First published by Zidane Press in 2009.

Copyright © Richard Orsborne 2009
Zidane Press
25 Shaftesbury Road
London, N19 4QW

The right of Richard Osborne to be identified as author has been asserted in accordance with Copyright, Design and Patents Act 1988. Any unauthorized broadcasting, public performance, copying
or re-copying will constitute an infringement of copyright. Permission granted to reproduce for
personal and educational use only. Commercial copying, hiring, lending is prohibited.

Cover design and photography by Anastasia Sichkarenko

Distributed by:
Turnaround Publisher Services Ltd
Unit 3
Olympia Trading Estate
London N2Z 6TZ
T: +44 (0)20 88293019

ISBN: 9780955485039

Biritish Library Catuloguing in Publication Data
A catalogue recod for this book is available from the British Library

UP THE BRITISH

Richard Osborne

Zidane Press

WANDSWORTH LIBRARY SERVICE

Introduction

The arguments about the nature of Britishness and British Identity have gone on at great length in many forums; the point of this book is not to review all of these debates but simply to set out as clearly as possible the basic themes that underpin them. This is not an academic book, nor a history book, it is a polemical work that sets out to confront some of the big ideas that are so taken for granted in the debates that it seems as though they really are truths; rather than fictions. The British have a peculiar kind of love affair with themselves which clearly puzzles many outsiders and needs some explaining. The aim of this book is to begin that process.

Chapter One
What Is Britishness?

The debate about Britishness is promoted by the extent of our post-war decline. We are no longer kept together by the need to fight wars, we are no longer all Protestants and we do not have the self-interest of belonging to a massive global empire.
Linda Colley, Historian

Britishness is newspapers, Marmite, pubs and the BBC – that is what people miss when they go abroad, and they must all be preserved and guarded jealously. It's also politeness – it's apologising, irony and self-mockery. It's speaking in codes and not saying what you mean, like telling someone "We must have lunch" when you can't stand them – unlocking those codes is getting to know what it is like to be British.'
Deborah Moggach, Novelist

This question of what it means to be British has always been a complicated topic, given that it is an imaginary identity made up of different ethnic groups and cultures, as well as an Empire. It has become a hotly debated topic during the last thirty years because

Britain is clearly changing rapidly and the settled way of life that we used to assume was quintessentially British, cultural things like roast beef, cricket, rain, stamp-collecting, whippets, the Empire and the Royal Family, has somehow changed into something else. These things are mostly still there but none of them seem the same, beef is dangerous because of mad-cow disease, cricket has become a global sport run by Australians and Indians and the Royal Family, apart from her good self, seem to be either barking, challenged, reactionary or peculiar. Except, of course, the blessed Princess Diana, who is a demi-god descended from Joan of Arc and Mother Theresa, combined with Kate Moss and Olivia Newton-John. The Princess Diana story is itself a tale of our times and one could look at all the contemporary cultural changes through this fairy-tale, but there are other things of importance. The idea that Britain was white, Christian and happily tolerant has been replaced with a sense that we are multi-cultural, multi-ethnic, much richer and yet much less happy or homogeneous. The problem is that the more the Brits want things to stay the same, the more impossible it seems, and this leads to a deep-seated contradiction in the British psyche.

There is a powerful nostalgia about the things we thought were British, and for a period when they were all simple, and a contradictory desire for everything that is rather different to the British thing, like foreign food and holidays, American culture and TV glamour. We want to have our cake, keep it preserved forever, then eat it and complain that it is stale and peculiar and foreign tasting. Being British is a rum business, and the confusion that we experience infects all politics, culture and sport, although in our amateurish way the sporting thing still seems to be consistent, as in we can't really win anything. Things are either wonderfully secure, like the Last Night of the Proms or bizarrely hopeless like the Millennium Dome and the glorious Terminal Five at Heathrow. Perhaps maintaining the balance between the clever and the incompetent is the key to British culture. Trying to work out how all these contradictory tensions are held together is the underlying issue this book will deal with.

It would be reasonable to say that currently the United Kingdom is going through something of an identity crisis, a little spasm when the Great in Great Britain feels more insecure and problematic than it has done for a very long time. What it means to be 'British' is contested and debated in ways that show a deep insecurity about the supposed core values and traditions that underpin our sceptred isle, or perhaps that should be sceptical isle. For example, recently the Chief Rabbi, Sir Jonathon Spears said in an extended interview with the *Telegraph* that basically Britain was losing its identity, and that this was because of 'over-zealous political correctness and a failure to deal with immigration.'[1] In this cheerful vein he went on to say 'that the drive for a multi¬cultural society had left Britain increasingly intolerant and that too many people were embarrassed about their history.' In an age in which the British are once again invading old Imperial countries just like we used to, and failing again, the idea of over-zealous political correctness seems a little whimsical. If he'd said over-zealous deranged fantasies of world domination and British superiority one might have been able to go along with him, but apparently political correctness now infests not just loony left councils but the British army and Gordon Brown (sometimes known as Tony Blair); as well as the White House. The rise of political correctness as a term of catch-all political abuse is in itself a symptom of a profound fear of contemporary change and of nostalgia for the past, when everything was sensible and sorted, and women knew their place (along with the 'coloured brethren').

As a country whose history is one of endless immigration, invasion and generally mongrel genetic background, it seems odd to talk about a failure to deal with immigration; perhaps we should expel everyone whose ancestors arrived before 1066, especially the Vikings. Immigration and refugees can quite conceivably be seen as the motor of cultural and intellectual energy in the British experience over the centuries so the supposed failure to deal with immigration is a rather odd idea. As a Nation that constantly went and visited, or some might say 'occupied' other countries it seems particularly perverse to object to outsiders coming in. As our troops execute something called the 'War on Terror' which sounds very like a crusade, it is worth remembering just how many countries we have invaded over the centuries, from Afghanistan to Zanzibar. In fact we have been invading Afghanistan for at least 150 years, on and off, and the net result has generally been rather a lot of dead people on both sides and not very much political correctness, or cultural advance. There was even a Carry On film lampooning our battles up the Khyber Pass which must mean that in some strange way it is officially part of British culture. The British part of the British Empire is actually a very interesting and complicated set of ideas and myths, and it is that underpinning of our contemporary culture that the Chief Rabbi is referring to when he says people are embarrassed about their history. How history and multiculturalism combine is really the question that has to be answered about contemporary Britain. The question is how come we are so obsessed with the heritage but refuse to confront the history?

These arguments by the Chief Rabbi go straight to the heart of the matter in bringing out the fact that Britain has changed a great deal since the Second World War and that many people find these changes unsettling and threatening. He went on to say, however that 'the historic Union with Scotland and the concept of Britain must be preserved.' which would seem to suggest that he knew what the concept of Britain was, which is more than many Brits seem to know. He also called for a 'British Day' when presumably everyone would go Morris dancing, drink warm beer and complain about the weather until they got so drunk they would start fighting over football, which seem to be the main cultural activities these days – except that everyone actually drinks ice-cold lager and Alco pops. On consideration, the idea of celebrating 'Britishness' is clearly quite silly since it is, at very best, a very vague set of ideas; rather like the Church of England and good manners. You can, for example, have a dog show because it is quite easy to define what is a dog and what isn't, defining the British is like asking five psychiatrists to define sanity.

There is an argument that attempting to define Britishness is quite pointless, and another that once it becomes a question it really shows that the whole thing has evaporated, which is why people feel troubled about it. (This is known as the Pandora's paradox.) There is merit in each of these arguments but in the end there is clearly something that people feel as 'Britishness' that has to be explored because it is the basis on which quite a lot of activities and energies are deployed. The point is that something that starts out as seemingly clear and obvious, we are 'British' as it were, quite rapidly becomes a difficult discussion about history, myth, nationality and culture, all topics that are notoriously difficult to deal with. The definition of the English is another slightly tricky question that gets subsumed into the Britishness thing, but in the wider general sense it is really much the same question. The character of the English and the British ideals overlap to such a great extent that it is almost, but not quite, the same. That the British idea is wider than the English is true, but the core of the mythology is an English idea, overlaid with togetherness, Empire and shared values. These shared values were those of Empire, class, collaboration and general superiority, and with the decline of the Empire it is not surprising that those mutually rewarding pacts have broken down. In thinking about Britishness however, it is necessary to point out that we are our history; this may be obvious but is trickier than you might think. The British Empire is actually the elephant in the room, as they say, and in more ways than one. It is the great shibboleth that lurks behind any discussion of Britain, and what it is and how it became what it is, (not to mention the real elephant, which came from the colonies and got shot by us, all of which we don't like to talk about). Having had an Empire for a very long time, and being the Top Dog in the world for quite a while, inevitably rubs off on one, and one tends to feel that being a White Man (and more specifically a British White Man) is rather the bees knees. Here is a quote from an advanced school reader in history from 1905 which pretty much sums up the Imperial ideology on which the whole thing was based.

Growth of the British Empire

The British Empire is in many respects the most wonderful the world has ever seen. It is the largest that has ever grown up on the globe, and in population, it is exceeded, if at all, only by the Chinese Empire. But its most marvellous feature is to be found, not in its size, but in its union of freedom, order and progress.[2]

The mixture of understatement and simultaneous claim to natural superiority in every respect is very indicative of the ways that the British saw themselves, and this neatly encapsulates many of the themes of this book. Racial superiority and cultural dominance went hand in hand, and it was our civilising mission, 'the white man's burden' that defined the British character over hundreds of years.

The British Empire, whilst embracing many lands and people of many colours, was actually quite white in its heart; it was simultaneously blue-blooded, multi-coloured and Persil white. That is why the legacy of the British Empire is clear as mud, or red, white and blue all over, with pink across the globe and black stripes across its bows, with purple bits where the royalty went. Colour, as some great painter once said, is in an important issue and one that raises questions around the British Empire which go beyond the burning question of what colour the drapes should be in the living room (or is that drawing room?)

One does not want to paint too nasty a picture of our forebears, nor to underestimate the progress that has been made, but really the question of white superiority actually has to be confronted, and the other, squeamish question of slavery which lurks below the surface. We are our history, and the history cannot be rewritten by re-assigning motives to various liberal Methodists who might have been anti-slavery in the early 19th century.

From Elizabeth I to Enoch Powell the assumption of British superiority mutated into a racial ideology which naturally assumed that white was superior and black inferior, and nobody put it more clearly, or more nostalgically, than Mr Powell in his nefarious speech known as the 'Rivers of Blood' speech. He carefully, and dishonestly, articulated the emotional hurt that the British felt after losing their superiority. He dressed it up as fact and analysis, but it was nothing more than a maudlin demand to go back to the good old days. Powell was very British in many ways, not least in his claim to honesty and uprightness combined with a venal hypocrisy that the Borgias would have approved of. The British capacity for self-delusion and hypocrisy in fact makes the Italians look like amateurs in the game of diplomacy; the British managed to rule the world and make people feel grateful for being exploited, not bad going for a bunch of gruff sea-faring types.

The Empire stretched all around the globe, lasted for hundreds of years and formed and fostered the British psyche in ways that still shape our reactions, thoughts, myths and means of thinking about ourselves. That is why we cannot avoid talking about it but somehow also want to ignore it as much as possible, except to remember the good bits; this is otherwise known as selective memory or the natural process of repressing the nasty bits. It also explains the very odd relationship the British have to their history. As the Chief Rabbi notes, many feel ashamed of it but the rest want to celebrate the expurgated movie version. Our finest hour is meant to exculpate the many months of rather nasty murdering of the natives over long periods, in many places and in many different ways; unfortunately one good speech does not silence three hundred years of bitter complaint. In short the contemporary attitude is something like: let's forget the past, forgive and forget, but let's celebrate our glorious history because it is so particular, but not in a way that might suggest we approved of nasty things like invading other people's countries, not that we ever did really, we were invited in, and anyway if we hadn't gone there the Germans would have done and they are so much worse. There is some exaggeration here but not as much as would first seem apparent. The earlier quote from the school reader conveys that sense that people wanted to foster, that somehow the British Empire was just natural and now we have wisely closed it down in an orderly manner. (This is big myth number 7) This strange set of ideas about our past could be described as post-imperial dementia, mixed with a soupcon of nostalgia and a large dose of rose-tinted Pimms.

This state of denial, or the polite hypocrisy for which the British are so elegantly equipped, basically argues that we really did quite a good job in the worst of all situations and anyway we gave back the colonies in the end so what is the problem, and we taught them to play cricket and so on. Not to put too fine a point on it, the British have a deeply schizophrenic attitude to their history and for very good reasons, and that profound ambivalence has continued right up to the present day when we have to deal with the consequences of Empire and immigration and really don't want to. This is the Gordian knot at the heart of British culture. Perhaps we can say that in terms of the culture everything that starts out seemingly clear, like beer and cricket and fairness all round soon becomes murky when you examine it closely, since all culture is in some way made up. What we need to look at is both how British history and culture got made up, from early origins in Chaucer and Shakespeare, how it was shaped in the twentieth century and how it functions now. We also need to examine the curious psychological dimensions of the British outlook, wherein they manage to conceive of themselves both as superior and somehow a victim of some nebulous plot. From Kipling through to Buchan and Fleming there is a interesting strain of perceiving the British as noble and upright in a wicked world, wherein the tough-minded but decent Brit (Hannay or Bond) thwarts the evil foreigners who are trying to destroy everything that is decent. This 'boy's own' version of the world is extraordinarily resilient and powerful, down to 'our boys' in Iraq being noble in helping the people in Basra. unlike the nasty Americans who kill people.

In thinking about the myths of Britishness Churchill obviously

9

embodies many of the things we are talking about, and he carefully crafted many phrases that resonate in the culture, like the 'our finest hour' speech, and the Dunkirk spirit and the British bulldog and fighting them on the beaches. For many he is synonymous with the British ideal. His career trajectory and attitudes are worthy of much consideration in thinking about the development of a certain phase of the British concept, and we shall come back to him quite often, not least because he also exemplifies certain slightly unsavoury traits that aren't as British as they could be. Criticising Churchill is akin to criticising the Monarchy, or Jesus, and that in itself reflects something about how powerful the myths of Britishness are; they are psychologically felt to be inviolable, untouchable and in this they are rather close to being a sort of secular religion. The strangeness of this emerged with the death of Princess Diana, when a national out-pouring of pseudo-religious grief engulfed the nation over the untimely demise of the 'People's Princess'. These feelings are deeply emotional, non-rational, and not about real communities but about an imaginary world that people occupy in their daydreams. Britain is, of course, an imaginary place and the values of Britishness are equally made up, but they function very well as a kind of social cement, or at least they did till recently. We are supposedly tolerant, fair-minded, liberal, honest and respect the rule of law and of justice in general, as well as being cultured, humorous and eccentric, valiant and stubborn. These are very noble traits and there is clearly nothing wrong with them, the question is how real are they, or were they?

Holding up the history to the light, and looking critically at what is going on now will answer some of these questions.

Reflecting on these issues Janet Daly in the recent debate about the idea of Britishness had this to say:

It is not the indoctrination of some mystical sense of Britishness that is required but a restoration of the quiet pride and conviction that used to enable Britons to maintain the highest standards of civil behaviour in the world. [3]

Nostalgia is never very far away in these discussions, most commonly and obviously with regard to the Second World War, but also to the Empire and the times when people knew their places. As John Major, one time Prime Minister famously put it, that in 50 years' time, Britain would still be the country of 'long shadows on county grounds, warm beer, invincible green suburbs, dog lovers and pools fillers and – as George Orwell said "old maids bicycling to holy communion through the morning mist".' This last image is so bizarre one presumes that John Major was indulging in that other British skill of irony; or just downright eccentricity. The fantasy of a rural Britain, of cute little villages where everyone knows everyone is so strong it seems to obliterate even the vaguest sense of reality in those who should know better. As the entire south-east gets tarmaced over for motorways and car parks for ghastly giant shopping centres so the myth of villages keeps growing; now we have urban villages where even the drug-dealers grow plants. Obviously most people live in big urban conurbations which are the exact opposite of cute little villages and the way they live bears as much relationship to the Archer's world as Gazza's lifestyle does. It is true that lots of people live in the suburbs, which are neither green nor invincible, more like grey and paranoid, but they are merely part of the urban sprawl which covers Britain with a density that is quite shocking, and shockingly uniform. The playing fields of Britain, on which the battles of Waterloo and other great away fixtures were supposedly won, have all been sold off to property developers so that the nearest most people come to the rural dream is driving through the clogged up tourist villages that are strategically placed not far from motorways. There is also the burning question of fox hunting which apparently is not to do with people chasing and murdering foxes but with a townie desire to stop wholesome country folk from doing something that is quintessentially British and generally good fun, as well as necessary. Suddenly the bucolic rural dream of oldie England turns into a snarling war of words between animal loving city greenie types and red-faced psychos in wellies. The British love of fair play seems to have gone the way of the local bobby on the beat and as in many walks of British life 'fings ain't what they used to be.'

It was said that the battle of Waterloo was won on the playing fields of Eton, which is odd because generally Waterloo is thought to be in Belgium or somewhere; perhaps we won because they were over there and we were here. However, this famous quote does raise another tricky little question about the nature of Britishness and that relates to the other problem that is always there and sometimes ignored, that of class. We British know where we belong, and whilst we may all be equally British, some of us are more equal than others. In a bitter debate in the House of Commons in 1941 about special treatment for the elite Public schools a Labour M.P. Charles Ammon argued that,

> *While it is said the Battle of Waterloo was won on the playing fields of Eton, it can be answered now that the Battle of Britain was won on the playing fields of the [State] schools of England.* [4]

The class battle between the elite private schools, like Eton and Harrow, which of course are called public schools in some kind of bad joke about access, and the newly emerging state-system is merely the most obvious way that class war is waged in Britain.

We are a country blessed with a Monarchy, an aristocracy, and a class system that is particularly slothful in changing itself over the centuries and, despite all appearances, not a great deal has changed in the 21st century. Atlee's post-war government thought about ending the elite, privileged education system that had run things for a very long time, but faced with a virtual civil uprising from the monied classes, decided to back down. The less diplomatic Labour M.P. Aneurin Bevan in the same debate said 'There is a great body of opinion, which isn't sufficiently articulate, that public schools should be allowed to die a natural death. Some would like them to die a little more violently.'[5] It was thought after the Second World-War that things were going to change dramatically and irrevocably, that the old way of doing things would die away, but the stubbornness that is supposed to be one of the British traits was in evidence here, for after a little flurry things seemed to go on as ever. Opportunity, education, money, life-chances and even health are all still completely unequally distributed across our social system, as every piece of research endlessly demonstrates, yet we persist in believing that this is the land of the fair, the broad-minded and the equal. Again the question remains why do we prefer, by far, to live in the fantasy world of 'Britishness' and repeat the mantra that we have the 'best education system in the world' when it is palpably falling apart, class ridden and not delivering what the economy, the individual or the culture, requires. In India they spend about 1/100th of what we spend per pupil on education and their numeracy and literacy rates are better and this is true in many other countries. There is something about the education system in Britain that is not quite what it appears to be; this whole question has to be thought about in some detail and we shall return to it later.

So what is 'Britishness', and is it polite to ask such a question? In a recent speech Gordon Brown, who has decided that national character is now a policy issue, which should scare everyone, had this to say about it. He said that the good things about us were our 'creativity, inventiveness, enterprise, our internationalism, our central beliefs in liberty for all, responsibility by all and fairness to all'. These are ideas that have been around for a while but then everybody likes to think they have these characteristics; nobody gets up and says we're curmudgeonly, xenophobic, introverted and miserable. If by Internationalism Gordon means our love of foreign holidays he is bang on, but if he means our love of Europe and our ability to speak and understand foreign languages then he is plainly indulging in porky-pies. The odd fact that he is Scottish, as are quite a few other politicians, and that the state of the Union is a bit frazzled, also underpins the peculiarity of going on about British values; one might think there was a problem somewhere. In fact Scottish nationalism is very much on the rise and the state of the Union has the kind of okey-cokey quality that Britain's membership of Europe displays, you put your right foot in, your right foot out, shake it all about, you do the okey-cokey, that's what it's all about. This kind of Britishness, where we join Europe and then pretend they bullied us into it and mistreat us at every opportunity, is straight from the Basil Fawlty school of internationalism, in which a morally superior Britain is somehow bamboozled by cunning foreigners. So once more as soon as you start to wheel out the obvious claims about the straightforward Brits and their no-nonsense, fair-minded view of the world it begins to unravel like Basil's best-laid plans. The fact that that we had Sybil as Prime Minister for years probably didn't help, but that's another story, made more intriguing by the number of M.Ps who professed love for 'Nanny' Thatcher. She was our first pro-Victorian, modernising, ruthlessly efficient, Tudor politician since Doctor Who, although she shared more characteristics with the Daleks than with the Time Lord. Again the serious point is that you can only modernise in Britain by pretending to go back to Victorian values, which were another set of strangely mythological ideas rooted in Empire; you can talk about modernisation but not about getting rid of the peculiar, class ridden, lop-sided almost feudal way of doing things in Britain. When Tony Blair goes on about modernising you know it will involve three things; bureaucracy, computers and packs of managerial bean-counters who can neither manage nor work computers. After several years of serial incompetence the name of the modernising campaign will be changed and it will all start again, 'four-eyes equal and forward to the integrated new-start new vision' will be the slogan, capped with a statistic that proves that standards have risen in the last eight years out of seven and doubled since Labour came to power. This New Britain is queerly Orwellian in many ways and so far from the myths of competence and harmony we are concerned with that one looks for the join in the parallel Universes. From Blair to Brown just reminds us that the Leader is always there, and watching you. Is Britain liberal, multi-cultural and progressive, or is it a society in terminal melt-down and driven by violence, drunkenness and no-go areas for Christians, as some newspapers would have us believe?

The history of the politics of Britishness, and of its mythic thinking, is rooted in our history, as everyone agrees, and that history is one of Empire, of domination, and of, if one dare use the word, exploitation. One must quickly add the word civilisation after this though, as we were always happy to dispense the latter as we marched around the globe. This imperial ideology of our 'civilizing mission' was a carefully concocted collection of ideas about how we would bring progress and prosperity to people by liberating them from superstition, giving them Christianity, and adding the benefits of science and commerce. It all sounded so reasonable and fair, but of course the real picture was rather darker and more oppressive, as well as very hypocritical. By this stage it is clear that we are talking about a rag-bag of associated ideas and images, different kinds of stereotypes that embed an outlook, an imaginary sense of being that is partly real, partly imaginary and absolutely, really more often observed in the breach rather than in the field. How these myths survived for so long is one of the mysteries of the 20th century; how they are kept alive with the oxygen of royalty, media and celebrity culture, along with the Heritage industry and the marketing of nostalgia is a matter of great interest. Britishness as a state of mind could perhaps be described as a very clever form of self-delusion, fortified with historical illusions, poetic memories and powerful institutions, but which is in a state of crisis precisely because it steadfastly refuses to confront reality as it now is. Centuries of such self-delusion may have formed the basis of this post-Imperial dementia.

At a debate about Britishness in 2004 organised by the RSA and the *Telegraph* newspaper, Kirsty Wark referred to a Mori poll about Britishness that had been conducted especially for the meeting, and had been done both at home and abroad. She said that it showed a less nostalgic view of Britain, but one in which the general perception was of individuality, humour and pride in the general idea of being British. She summed up the results:

> *They paint a picture of a tolerant, polite, slightly reserved nation of free-spirited individuals who are politically independent and possess an excellent sense of humour, a very clever sense of humour indeed, many of our overseas' focus groups said* [6]

This idea of tolerance is central to Britain's self definition but it is a very particular kind of tolerance, which currently doesn't seem to extend to immigrants, Muslims, radicals and anyone else who isn't quite right. Throughout British history tolerance has actually been of the stay in your place and you can enjoy yourself, but get out of line and we'll thrash you severely variety. The idea of the aristocracy, which is at the heart of the British Empire outlook, and of royalty itself, is a deeply reactionary and genetically exclusive ideology which is savagely intolerant. If one looks at the reaction to the Labour victory in 1945, the upper classes became completely hysterical about how a communist government would destroy everything that was British.[7] Churchill himself claimed that the Labour party in 1945 was merely a communist front and that Atlee 'would have to fall back on some form of Gestapo' in order to bring into being his socialist aims. Despite Labour winning by a landslide the upper classes were so tolerant they claimed the country was ruined, the Empire finished and that disaster threatened everyone. Mrs Thirkell, a popular novelist of the day wrote in her book *Private Enterprises* concerning the Labour Government:

> *What I really mind is their trying to bust up the Empire... I mean like leaving Egypt and trying to give Gibraltar to the natives. If they try to do anything to Gibraltar, I shall put on a striped petticoat and a muslin fichu and murder them all in their baths, because TRAITORS ought to be murdered.* [8]

That is one of the finest definitions of tolerance it is possible to come by, and on a par with British football hooligans' views of what to do to foreigners when one loses in the World cup, as one inevitably does. The delightful Mitford family also quite nicely demonstrate how tolerance was such a key attribute of upper-class life in Britain, from the mad father who didn't think girls should be educated to Diana, who married the fascist Mosely and Unity, who probably had an affair with Hitler and then shot herself when we went to war with the nice Germans. The slightly less barking Nancy wrote several books including the one in which she outlined her famous creation of the concept of 'U' and 'Non-U', a theory she borrowed and developed in her book *Noblesse Oblige* and in many newspaper articles. In this work she attempted to convey the idea of proper English usage; with 'U' standing for correct usage, and 'Non-U' for incorrect 'Napkin' was 'U' whereas 'serviette' was Non-U. 'Lavatory' was 'U' but 'toilet' or 'loo' most definitely was not, in other words she was describing how to be posh.[9] All frightfully funny and not at all an intolerant joke about how the lower orders spoke, (or should that be spoked). The point here is that tolerance was nowhere to be seen in the relations between the classes in Britain, except when the lower orders were needed to go off to war and die in their thousands, in which case much was made of their chummy and cheerful Britishness.

Throughout the days of the Empire the rigid class distinctions in the British army and Navy were rigidly enforced, often with catastrophic results like the Charge of the Light Brigade, something that James discusses at length in his *The Rise and fall of the British Empire*.[10] The upper classes in British history have been so well known for their love of the lower classes, as many novelists have demonstrated from Dickens to D.H. Lawrence, from Orwell to Irvine Walsh, that one wonders where the stereotypes come from. Class is probably thicker than water, and blood definitely is. One might be equal but some are just a little bit more equal than others.

The story that Britain developed through a happy commingling of peoples after the Romans left and by some warmly organic process grew into a peaceful, harmonious realm through the Tudor era and into the British Empire, in which tolerance and fairness ruled supreme, is pretty much just that, a story. The myths of Britishness were as carefully constructed as the warships we used to pulverise our opponents and as the ideologies we used to indoctrinate ourselves and those lesser mortals to whom education was only granted after we left. The British Empire was a truly great affair, but it was in truth a rickety apparatus organised to maximise profit, encourage trade and ensure British supremacy of the high seas and the low forms of exploitation. God may have been on our side but, like Nelson, he appears to have had a blind eye when it came to certain moral deficiencies. What this story is really about is coming down from the highs of Imperial exploitation and confronting reality as an everyday capitalist nation, rather than as the moral arbiter of world civilisation and politics. The morning after the night before is rarely a time of happy memories and bold energies, and delusion often sets in before lunch time, that is why the Brits still hanker after 'elevenses' or cocktails and shall there be honey for tea. The story really begins with the Elizabethan order, with Raleigh and the Navy, with the burgeoning sense of a nation and with all things British, like Shakespeare and Kipling.

Indeed the Tudor era has long been associated by literary historians with the 'discovery of England' – the process by which the English/British people became proudly conscious of their national language, geography, history and destiny. These myths of origins are poetic constructions but they reverberate through the national consciousness like the chimes of Big Ben, and images and myths are always more powerful than history, truth and logic.

Lawrence James, in his quite underrated book *The Rise and Fall of the British Empire* summarizes all of this in the following way:

In one sense "Britishness" could not be detached from the imperial past. It had largely been fabricated to strengthen national unity during the wars against France in the eighteenth and early nineteenth century. The Union of England, Wales, Scotland and Ireland and the cohesion it imposed was vital during that period of imperial growth. Indeed Scotland's entry into the Union in 1707 was in large part determined by a widespread urge to share in the overseas commercial advantages hitherto enjoyed by England alone. The Union gave Scots access to colonies, tropical markets and, in time, commissions in imperial armies and posts in imperial governments.

However as Patrick Wright also put it so well some years ago, in his discussion of 'Everyday Life, Nostalgia and the National Past in his *On Living in an Old Country*;

Cultural manipulation pervades contemporary British society – not least in endless public invocations of the national identity and tradition, and there is a lot to be said about it.[11]

The following chapters will have quite a lot to say about it.

Chapter Two
The Stories We Tell Ourselves

Britain's gnawing hunger for retrospection is of Proustian proportions; historical confections of past glory are always being sugared up and nibbled at somewhere in the land.
Francis X. Clines, Historian

The history of any country is a fairy tale told in reverse, we make up later the stories that explain how we became the wonderful nation we are; at first they are myths and later they become facts. The British idea of historical truth is a tale that is one of extraordinary continuity, lack of invasion, chivalrous behaviour, happy endings and ridiculous good luck. (It is really the story of the hobbit with a garden shed) It is a simple tale, well-told and often repeated, but unfortunately the ending has gone somewhat pear-shaped, disorganized and quite unlike endings are supposed to be; however we persist with the stories we are most fond of, those of plucky good luck and gentlemanly what-ho. From Boedicia, King Arthur via good Queen Bess, Robin Hood, Francis Drake, Doctor Livingstone, Queen Victoria and the Second World War the tale is one of quiet bravery against the odds, like the Armada over and over again. Keeping calm and pulling together, whilst puffing on a pipe are pretty much the standard moods of historical experience;

heroism, health and horticulture combine so that Britain will never be defeated and all that. Here's a journalist discussing the diary of a First World War Officer;

> *It is full of Blackadder-ish moments, including Stewart's annoyance at having to put down his pipe because the smoke was getting in the way of shooting Germans.* [1]

Being British is a state of mind and it mostly involves feeling united, superior, and evangelical all at once, combined with plenty of smoke and mirrors. God, as is well known, is also an Englishman, which explains why the Church of England prefers sherry to religion, and why pipes are so important.

Ironically now of course, the divisions between the constituent parts of Britain- England, Ireland, Scotland and Wales, have never been greater, yet the commitment to the idea of Britishness remains strong. Britain is such a powerful idea simply because the patterns of the mythology have had so long to take root and grow, shielded by the hedgerow, the sea and the geographical closeness of the communities that occupied these isles. Sailing, singing, drinking and being a friendly chap, and loving one's little corner of this bucolic isle, and respecting one's neighbour's eccentricities are the generally unspoken rules of this sepia-tinted nirvana. These stories of a Britain always at ease with itself don't stand up to the slightest investigation however, and are patently delusional at another. Britons have almost always been at war with each other, and if not war then pretty serious disagreement. From the Wat Tyler rebellion in 1381 against the savage oppression of peasants, though the Civil War of 1641-1652, the Jacobite rebellions of 1715, the Chartist battles of the 1840s, the Tolpuddle Martyrs, the rise of unions and the Labour Party, the history of Britain is one of a subdued class war that defined power, privilege and control of an immensely rich global empire. If you think back to Thatcher's mobilization of the Britishness myth it involved thrashing the Argies, but also thrashing the miners who, as far as one knows, were probably British. The vitriol invoked then hardly displays a cuddly unity of purpose, and Thatcher alluded to it as civil war at one point and the miners as 'traitors' – hardly the stuff of togetherness. Similarly in the 1926 General Strike, miners battling for a pathetically low minimum wage were constantly described as Bolsheviks, communists and criminals. Churchill of course was adamant that unions had to be smashed by almost any means as they posed a threat to the unity of the Empire.[2] He was convinced that the strike was a prelude to a communist Revolution, so much faith did he have in his British compatriots (or understanding of reality).

In order to engineer internal peace Britain was also almost continually at war with external enemies, which always has the effect of making the home front more cohesive, or seemingly so. Perhaps the greatest achievement of the British Empire was its means of convincing the British hordes that serving the Empire was something that everyone had a stake in, and that common principles embraced us all. George Orwell understood this better than anyone, and some of the aims of his great novel *1984* (and *Animal Farm*) are actually to do with the great British gift of propaganda, the ability of an elite to hoodwink the lower orders for most of the time, if not all of the time. It may be the greatest contribution of the aristocracy to world history, particularly since there is no evidence of any contribution anywhere else. The myth of an endlessly harmonious Britain does not stand up to the smallest historical reflection, indeed from the earliest beginnings there was a recognition of difference and antagonism. However as one commentator put it rather succinctly:

From time immemorial societies have formed around their
myths and heroes. There has never been a society where
this was not the case. They are the principal means by which
the individual becomes tied in to a common identity. [3]

The trouble with myths and heroes is that they become carved in stone and eventually end up making change and progress difficult, as well as rendering people blind to the realities of everyday life. Since the high-point of the Second World-War Britain has been in a state of denial, of dissaffection and slow and complicated decline, all designed to blur the terriible truth that we mostly don't like each other, never mind strangers. When the British aren't being rude about foreigners they like to moan about their neighbours and indeed moaning, rather than loving, is probably one of the key attributes of the British. The strange British attitude to children exemplifies this, they are always seen as a problem rather than the gift of the future.

Historically speaking, division has always been the order of the day. The British genius has always been to cobble something together that looks like harmony, and to work very hard at the business of myth-making. Here's an historian commenting on the early Britons that sets the scene. 'The Britons who lived in the south were not so rude and ignorant as those who dwelt further north'[4] referring to the Ancient Britons who were around before the Romans, Druids, Saxons, Jutes and all the other various types who made up the early population, but one can see that prejudices make good copy. The Romans thought the British were pretty much demented hooligans and so again, history does seem to repeat itself, or at least you can't keep a good story down.

The difference between stories and history is that the former begin 'Once upon a time' and the latter begin 'In the time of' and then they converge as history succumbs to the lure of the good story. This is a little unfair because historians do try and find facts to back up their theories, but then politicians take the theories and run with them, irrespective of facts. A lot of our early history comes out of the undisputed reality that the Romans were definitely here and definitely ran things, and since they recorded it we have something of a clear picture. As soon as they left we reverted to making things up on a grand scale, particularly the idea we always battled against the Romans and drove them out, rather than they had just had enough.

The opposition to the Romans gave us Boedicia, who was Mrs Thatcher in a chariot, and who hailed from the same flatlands of Lincoln, and bossed everyone around, but the similarity more or less ends there. Boadicia apparently had masses of red hair, was clearly a Celt and sacked Colchester and London, although there are those who argue Thatcher sacked the Greater London Council and fought running battles with the Patrician elites in much the same way. The immediate point is that historical images are always used and reproduced to link the present with the past and to provide a story of continuity that makes it all fit. Thatcher sometimes tried to present herself as Elizabeth, and sometimes as Churchill, but that was going a bit far. However the image of Elizabeth 'the Virgin Queen' is still a very potent image in contemporary culture, witness the endless films and television adaptations of her life, which is precisely how the history is kept alive. Our current Queen, Elizabeth II, carefully nurtures the historical links, and the idea that Monarchy is as natural as breathing infuses the great British culture, which, it is often pointed out, is unique. This carefully cultivated feeling of overwhelming 'pastness' and continuity is a very interesting cultural device, which has been so effective it has kept the great Elizabethean show on the road for far longer than was really viable. It is this out-of-dateness that is really becoming the problem, like British cars, British manufacturing and the whole crumbling, wheezing political edifice (not to mention the legal system and its supposed superiority).

The other key point about Elizabeth I, and the cult of Elizabethiania and Shakespearism, is that it all marks the beginning of the Protestant British outlook, of the Navy as a key instrument of policy and the beginnings of the Empire, or in other words of the modern British character (using 'modern' in the sense of post-feudal). Henry VIII also has an important role in all this as the jolly, boozing, down-to-earth inherently Protestant, rumbustious, anti-Papal, forceful, hunting-loving,super-sized English Squire who started it all off. He is another archetype we imbibe with our mother's milk and which is reinforced constantly with media adaptations, films, books and references to Falstaff, poems, and general Tudorisms, which are a set of ideas about the particularly British/Protestant anti-Catholic nature of our full-blooded first proper King (proper as in the sense of being jolly British). Henry wanted the Union with Scotland, saw the need for a powerful navy and understood that opposition to Catholicism meant a uniquely British scheme of things, so there is a proper sense in which he was the first British King.[5] It was the beginning of the British brand, one of the most successful media campaigns in all history. Brand values, as every advertiser will tell you, are key in keeping the consumer happy, and this brand was the first to get a global release, which gave it first principle status.

The dissolution of the monasteries, and the break with Rome, was the beginning of the cultural transformation of Britain into the Protestant, semi-secular, civil state that laid the foundation for the

British Empire and the modern version of Britishness. Interestingly, one of the strategies that Henry and Elizabeth followed was to be a popular monarchy, a very different model to the haughty, removed, virtually deified European model, where the gap between the people and the monarch was exaggerated rather than broken down. This populist bond, a carefully cultivated communality of purpose, has been an important asset in the survival of the monarchy in Britain. It wasn't the Americans who invented PR it was the Tudors and particularly Elizabeth, who perfected the sound bite five hundred years before the invention of television gave it its proper home (and recorded the coronation of the new Elizabeth model). Many of the themes that emerge from the Elizabethan era were given voice by Shakespeare and that process is in itself important, the literary was to play a significant role throughout the development of the Britishness idea. Shaping national myths is one of the roles of the writer and poet, and from Chaucer through William himself, Mallory, Johnson and up to Kipling, Buchan, Priestley, Orwell, T.S.Eliot et al it has been a whizz-bang business with stereotypes flying in all directions and polished myths being burnished by the fireside. You need good values to keep a brand afloat, and polishing the family myths and stories is what keeps up a good front. Briton's tend to dream in permanent nostalgia mode, tinged with a self-regard that became a key aspect of Empire self-certification; somehow we were good because we believed in goodness, just like fairies and unicorns.

If you think about the cultural images that are bandied about there is a great deal that refers back to our glorious maritime history and the time of buccaneering, gallantry and fighting the Spanish. One of the earliest tales that is taught in school is that of the Armada, good old Francis Drake and the bowling on the green scenario, or it might have been on the cliffs. Like a proper British/English gent he calmly finished his game of bowls, puffed on his pipe, strolled down to the ship and thrashed the Spanish without even breaking into a sweat or raising his voice. Obviously this is a true account of what actually occurred and everyone lit bonfires and went hurrah! From children's comics to television repeats and endless film epics the repetition of these stories builds collective memories, things that have psychic depth without any necessary factual basis. As Orwell observed, the endless repetition of stories turns fantasy into fact, and like other addicts people find it very hard to wean themselves off the stuff. Poetry may be even more addictive than stories, and hymns even stronger still. When *Blackadder* and *Monty Python* send all this up it is the strength of the myths that gives the satire its potency, and further down the track *Dad's Army* and *Hallo, Hallo,* repeat the same humourous tribute to Hobbitsville. Given the choice between fact and fiction most people unerringly choose fiction, which is perhaps a choice of the privileged. Later the plucky little Brits myth was then attached to the Battle of Britain, which was basically a re-run of the Armada in the air. The Falklands was simply Armada 3, a film repeat with John Geilgud, Trevor Howard and Thatcher as Elizabeth, and a lot penguins for extras.

To get back to the history, we can see Francis Drake as another important role model for the later British Empire. Whatever else he was Francis Drake was a privateer, or in other words a state sanctioned pirate who attacked the Spanish, got what he could and gave some of it to the Crown; that he was extremely successful at it makes it all the more commendable. Funnily enough he appears to be a bit of a Celt as well, and by all accounts rather wild and daring, rather like an early version of Errol Flynn. This free-enterprise, free-booting, practically lawless buccaneering clearly sounds like fun but it is hardly the gentlemanly activity that is written into the later stories. According to the Heritage history website

Sir Francis Drake is possibly the most illustrious pirate in world history ...He was an Admiral in the English Navy and second in command during the Great Armada, but most of his career was spent robbing, pillaging and wreaking havoc on Spanish war fleets, Spanish merchant fleets, and Spanish colonies in the new world. [6]

This British ability to take on the Spanish, to beat them at their own game, and to make up the rules at the same time, whilst then white-washing the entire enterprise as God-fearing and noble, demonstrates an interesting use of the cultural narrative to produce a damn good story, something that perhaps is more central to the discussion of the British Empire than might meet the eye. A good example of this tendency can be found in *Our Island Story: A history of England for Boys and Girls* by H. E. Marshall (1905), a gloriously funny story book replete with all the minor heroics that reappear in school books, comics, films and all the marvellous propaganda from our halcyon Imperial days. Here is Marshall on King Arthur, our greatest myth and also probably the one with the least historical basis of them all.

In those fierce and far-off days, when men spent most of their time fighting, it was very necessary for them to be brave and strong, in order to protect their dear ones, but they were very often cruel as well and nearly always fierce. Arthur taught people that it was possible to be brave yet kind, strong yet gentle. Afterwards people forgot this again, but in the days of Arthur the fame of his court and of his gentle knights spread far and wide.

Many commentators have noted the importance of the Arthurian legend in the mythological nexus of the British self-regard, this kindly but firm Christian ethos that was called upon in defining the gentleman-warrior of the British Empire, always doing the right thing even by the turbulent foreigners.

Marshall is almost too good to be true in the propaganda stakes, and just for entertainment she ends the Arthur section by saying:

Other people say the stories about Arthur and his knights are not true, but at least we may believe that in those far-off, fierce, fighting days there was a king who taught his people that to be gentle was not cowardly and that to be cruel was not brave.

There is virtually no evidence whatsoever of Arthur's existence and the round table but that is, as they say, a bit previous; if we all believe hard enough he'll come back to life. In a scholarly study of the origin and development of the Arthurian legend Adam Levin looks at the creation of the story, and of its literary and historical realities, in which the literary is by far the most important.

From the very beginnings of the English language there have been legends of great heroes. From the first settlements of Britain come stories rooted in ancient Celtic and Germanic imagination. Out of these stories, certain figures enjoy pre-eminence as the strongest, the bravest and the best. King Arthur is one such hero, known perhaps over all other mythical medieval figures as a chivalrous knight, a powerful warrior and a just and intelligent leader. [7]

The emergence of the idea of King Arthur, the Christian Knight who resists the pagans and insists on gentlemanly behaviour at all times becomes an important and powerful myth from medieval royal propaganda right through to Tennyson's Imperial ode *Morte D'Arthur* and the comics and films of the 20th century. (*Lord of the Rings* is really just a jazzed up version of Arthurian ideas.) The comprehensive story of King Arthur was first developed in literature by Geoffrey of Monmouth, a monk of Welsh origin, in *Historia Regum Britanniae* (The History of the Kings of Britain) – completed in about 1138 (in Latin) and then worked and re-worked by endless poets, authors and propagandists. This is what is meant by the convergence of history and myth.

The curious thing about understanding history, and historical myths, is that as soon as you start examining them they tend to evaporate into the 'mists of time' and the strange regions of collective fantasy and delusion that constitute living cultures. History is really just a set of very old newspaper stories that we recycle in ways that make us feel more secure, it is an exercise in nostalgia combined with contemporary ways of thinking about things; that is why history has to be re-written all the time. If you have one fact, like 'the Normans invaded in 1066', you then add about six dollops of fantasy, three quarts of myth, and two pints of strong British ale, and lo and behold, you have a well-cooked historical lunch, or beef in ale pie a la Normanesque. Here's Mark Twain talking about the western world's first historian, or the first one we know about.

> *Herodotus says, "Very few things happen at the right time, and the rest do not happen at all: The conscientious historian will correct these defects."* [8]

British historians are no better then anyone else in this regard, correcting defects all over the place, but because we write so much history it seems to be a more substantial thing than just stories.

Perhaps because we have hundreds of old buildings that represent the history, people think it is more real, it is 'sermons in stones' of a particular kind. Because Britain is so quaintly dotted with ancient ruins and well-preserved country houses, as well as castles and follies and other assorted historical stuff, and because it is all so prettily packaged, we appear to believe in it more powerfully. In some strange corner of our country's field we believe that our myths are more real, and more concretely grounded than everyone else's. People in Britain constantly say things like 'We British have always done so-and-so – the British legal system is the best in the world – or Britain is the most civilised country in the world' and that is the basis of another collective love in which an Imperial ideology dressed up as a sensible truth is wallowed in. The British have developed a form of myth that not only disguises itself, it disguises the very idea of mythology. Constant mysticism leads to a state of mystic denial in which the everyday gets confused with the mythic. This is what is meant by 'phlegmatic mysticism.'[9]

To approach it in another way, think of ideas such as; in times of any emergency have a cup of tea, that well-known Chinese thing that arrived here via India; or drink some wine to celebrate, that well-known middle-eastern thing that came via France. We are so British that our favourite food is curry, we drink European lager and wine, or ruminate over tea or coffee and think the potato is quintessentially British, whilst thinking we influenced everyone else. When the British talk of the Royal family they do so in a way that suggests it is simply a natural, perfect, god-given, real and sensible thing; unlike strange foreign dynasties that have been thrown out or discredited. That the Royal Family are basically German, aristocratic and in-bred never seems to bother anyone, nor the fact that the idea of Royalty is patently absurd, nineteenth century and inimical to democracy. Here again British fantasies are, like British engineering, copper-bottomed, clear and not at all fanciful. The problem really is that it is a question of how in particular we live in our myths, the way we have of inhabiting the stories we delude ourselves with, and a British way of generally behaving. Being British is a state of mind, and one that is most curiously peculiar. I have described it elsewhere as being 'phlegmatic mysticism' or a kind of down-to-earth sensibility that is both seemingly serious and mildly barking at the same time.[10] Just as every country has its particular myths and stories, so every country has its own way of 'being' in itself, and the British way of life, or sensibility, has developed slowly and solidly over many centuries. That it is so ancient, and untroubled, makes it seem all the more real, but as the tides of Empire waned so the rock like certainties of character in fact turned out to be shifting sands and delusional digressions. When India gained independence in 1947 the great white myth started to falter and has staggered from one attack to another ever since; and now the Scots want to get out and start their own business. The question really is how was the great British myth of 'fair-play', honesty and gentlemanly superiority kept afloat for so long, and why does it sill persist?

Here is a blogger defending the great British myth industry, and in so doing quite rightly pointing to the way that these collective fantasies drive a people's culture and organization.

One of the problems with Britain is that its mythology has been derided and contested by those who do not understand the importance of myth to a collective identity. Whether or not the British brought an end to slavery of Africans is perhaps less important than the impetus to nobility that the belief generates in succeeding generations. Some myths seek to explain our presence here, many religious myths taking this form, while others inspire, regimental and military mythology for example.

This blogger sums it up rather well, myths are a necessary part of the cultural functioning of any nation state and sustaining them is an integral part of keeping the 'national identity' whole, an activity that is always threatened by history, events and politics. Britain's peculiar mode of myth-making may be one of its key strengths, one shrouded in the mist of continuity and the security of belief; but sometimes waking up is also necessary.

The critical point is that in the process of myth-making, the production, dissemination and recycling of myths, the British have, probably since Elizabeth I and Shakespeare, been world-leaders in the business and, whilst others have gone in for painting, music or engineering, we have developed the most advanced form of self delusion known to humanity.

That Ian Fleming, a terribly British type altogether, invented James Bond, the world's silliest stereotype since Robin Hood, exactly delineates how this cultural machinary operates. When all around you are losing their heads, the trick is to describe the donward spiral of historical irrelevance as being sensibly British.

Being British is not straightforward, nor is the rise and fall of the notion of Britishness, rather than Englishness, but inventing the Nation is a process that requires work and commitment, and the British have a peculiarly peristant commitment to the work of mythologizing. In her seminal work *Britons: Forging the Nation. 1707 – 1837* Linda Colley summarises her position thus:

Even in the eighteenth and early nineteenth centuries, there were those who feared that the British identity was

too dependent on recurrent Protestant wars, commerical
success and imperial conquest, and that more thought
and attention should be devoted to consolidating a deeper
sense of citizenship on the home front [11]

This was to be the pattern for the next two centuries and a great deal was done to bolster up the British identity in cultural terms, persuading Welsh, English, Scottish and a few Irish that we were all in it together. The British brand was a kind of corporate management model, everyone in the company profits by pulling together and being a world leader but staying at the top always gets harder. Being British meant being at the top of the corporate global world, but as every business knows staying at the top comes up against the fifth law of physics. If things can go wrong, they will.

Empires come and go, from the Aztec to the Ottoman, and the process is mysterious; the only known truth is that power shifts and cannot be retrieved. The Story of Britishness has ended not with a bang but with a whimper.

Chapter Three
From Armada To Empire

Britishness as we know it today is really an idea of character that began to emerge in Tudor times, got bound up with Protestantism and then was further elaborated in the process of building an empire; that is why it emerged as an idea of a white, Christian, refined and superior warrior class that naturally set itself apart, and above, everyone else. Anti-catholicism turned into an integral part of this special identity, which was anti-European and in many ways isolated from the other main world powers. This separateness, and later reactions to European revolutions and intellectual ferment historically, came to define many of the aspects of Britishness. When successful it was an unbeatable formula, in decline it sets the seeds of British schizophrenia and post-Imperial maladjustment, as is now emerging. In earlier times it was however simply the definition of what it meant to be superior.

For the first three-quarters of the nineteenth century Britain appeared as a colossus astride the world. Britain dominated every field of human activity and its people seemed to possess an almost demonic energy. [1]

How and why the British came to be so dominant is an intriguing question that is constantly argued about and which won't be settled here. What we are more interested in is the ways in which the historical shaped what came to be known as Britishness. Whilst the factual history of things is fascinating in itself, here we are more concerned with the imaginary history that constitutes such a large part of nationalist mythologies. The relationship between history and myth is probably the central question of all cultural analysis, and is particularly important when thinking about empires and their necessary self-glorification. It is perhaps the demonic energy committed to mythologizing that kept the British Empire afloat for so long, and led to the difficulties of adjusting when it began to decline. The rise and fall of empires has been a continual cycle since the beginnings of culture, from the Babylonian to the contemporary American Empire, and the reasons are complex; the slow decline of the British Empire has been interesting because it is so obvious and yet so resented and resisted. Indeed it might be the case that the mythological British Empire was greater than the actual, on the ground, factual one. Believing in things, as religion proves, is a very powerful force in human affairs and it is the belief in Britishness that we are interested in. At some level the idea of national character, or national values, is clearly imaginary, but it is fascinating to see how the idea itself works.

British identity is inextricably bound up with our Imperial past, the reality of a global empire and the post-Imperial decline and fall; to avoid this truth is like America trying to ignore the reality of slavery, and they are bound together in mutual amnesia. Post-Imperial menopause was one term used to describe Britain's peculiar state and, whilst somewhat crude, it has an oddly useful feel for describing contemporary reality. This chapter will look at some of the ways that we arrived at an Imperial identity and how it still resonates today. It is a story that goes from Tudor hearts of oak to Powell's Rivers of Blood, and we are still contesting those deeply contradictory myths. The interesting question is what forces shaped the patterns of British identity and how are they different to other cultures, and why does it still resonate? To start at an obvious point.

> 'Rule Britannia, Britannia rules the waves,
> Britons never, ever shall be slaves.'

When patriotic crowds belt out this precise anthem to the past at the *Last Night of the Proms* you know you are in the realms of the historical and the mythic, the collective folk memory of the Empire. Most of the important events in Britain, like the opening of Parliament, the Trooping of the Colour, coronations and Royal weddings, garden parties, and military parades and tattoos etc are all based around the nostalgic memory of past glory and the sense of everlasting tradition. British identity is firmly rooted in the collective idea of history, of continuity and of things just being as they always have been. Ironically, of course, most of these traditions were really invented in the nineteenth century.[2] But they drew on and embellished traditions and ideas that were developed throughout the life of the British Empire. The process of transforming cultural stereotypes into accepted traditions is one that developed slowly during the life of the Empire, but which accumulated gravitas as each century rolled past. The accretion of centuries of culture builds a patina of certainty over the things of Empire, and, like the Monarchy they come to seem as timeless and unquestionable. This process is akin to what has earlier been called 'phlegmatic mysticism'.[3] What this means is that in the long and mostly uninterrupted process of the development of the British Empire an ideology grew up which was both a rationale for the Empire, the idea of civilizing the world, and an ever-growing belief in the destiny of the British, as chosen by God. That they neatly fitted together and justified Britain's taking over other territories is part of the brilliance of the whole enterprise. It wasn't a blatant triumphalism but more of a dogged determination to be top dog and to be quietly mystical about the 'white man's burden' Kipling of course captured this exactly in his poem of the same name (1899)

Take up the White Man's burden —
Send forth the best ye breed —
Go bind your sons to exile
To serve your captives' need...'

The claim is that we did it for the natives, for the sake of Christianity, and for the greater good of man, because we were the best breed or as the entrepreneurs said 'we'll have a piece of that.' Self-belief and self-delusion are close comrades and the British almost had a world monopoly on both. The character of the British is precisely that kind of phlegmatic mysticism which conceives of itself as down to earth but which is as quietly delusional as other nationalisms, only without the chutzpah. Aristocratic leadership combined with buccaneering morality plus a touch of religion and a soupcon of liberalism was a world-beating formula finely honed over decades of 'exploring' the world and trading with anyone and everyone.

When Francis Drake was out buccaneering he described it as being for Queen and country but that was the thinnest veneer of altruism; only in the later years did free trade become a religion and white supremacy simply a matter of fact. So, if we are beginning with the Tudors, the Navy and the protestant monarchy we can trace a path of cultural development that leads from buccaneering to the Great British Identity. This reached its apogee in Victorian times and only began to seriously erode after the Second World War. Our warrior tradition clearly relates to the fact that the British were always fighting wars, that the armed forces were central to the Empire and that violence (otherwise known as keeping law and order) was something that the British were particularly good at. 'Doing one's duty' was almost the catchphrase of the Empire and generally meant fighting to maintain Britain's dominance in any corner of the globe, and in ways that combined brutal power with brilliant cultural assimilation. Hierarchy, hypocrisy, propaganda and brutality were combined with brilliant seamanship, clever politics and a seemingly endless stream of good luck. Many wars initially went very badly, and British leadership was often appalling, but somehow the battles were eventually won and the Empire always muddled through.

From the Armada onwards the Navy, and its power, was to be the bedrock of British development and the model on which most of the Empire's forms and traditions would be based. The British Empire was impossible to conceive other than as the result of maritime expansion. From the seventeenth century onwards new maritime strength underpinned the development of an international trade network and an informal framework to support that trade, thus was a semi-privatized British Empire evolved. It is interesting to note that public-private initiatives were from the very beginning the basis of the development of the Empire. The Navy was eventually known as the Senior Service and its glory and pomp featured highly in the affections of the British people as a whole. Its importance was noted by Peter Borsay:

Up until 1797 Britannia was conventionally depicted holding a spear, but as a consequence of the increasingly prominent role of the Royal Navy in the war against the French, and of several spectacular victories, the spear was replaced by a trident... The navy had come to be seen... as the very bulwark of British liberty and the essence of what it was to be British. [4]

These themes of Brittannia, of what it represented of daring do and of our plucky navy battling against the odds recur over and over again in the mythological history of the British Empire, and are then repeated both in the Second World War and in the Falklands. The idea of the Island Nation struggling against a hostile world comes to define this central idea of Great Britain and was carefully evoked by the Thatcher government in its staging of the Falklands homecoming. Doing one's duty and protecting the nation are key themes in the entire empire tradition and the naval symbolism was an important leitmotif, always drawing on the Christ-like image of Nelson (who was a sort of sea-faring King Arthur). The naval patterns of discipline, hierarchy and natural leadership were combined with the right to rule of a landed aristocracy to produce the pomp and circumstance of the Great British Empire Show. Admirals and dukes, pomp and circumstance and, most of all Monarchy, symbolically came to represent the 'family' of the Empire, with the aristocracy as the parents of a huge and messy brood who had to be kept in order, for their own sakes.

In the Act of Union 1707 the Scottish Navy was amalgamated with the English and thus the Royal Navy was born, the instrument of British economic, military and cultural dominance throughout the next 250 years.

The Battle of Trafalgar 1805, in which the smaller British navy routed the French and Spanish navies, put the seal on Britain's global dominance which basically lasted until the First World War.[5] Trade, influence and dominions are what made the British

Empire so great and the basis of that greatness was precisely sea-power, and the discipline that made it possible. It is not too far-fetched to say that order, discipline and rigid hierarchies became the formal and psychological basis of the very idea of Britishness, something that was codified in the system of public schools in the eighteenth century. The class system in Britain transformed the declining peasantry into soldiers, sailors and industrial workers to provide the workforce of the Empire, and the cannon-fodder of Imperialism. It was a system that was unique, dynamic and culturally configured to produce a sense of inclusiveness, racial harmony and unity in the face of all external opposition. In this it was hugely successful.

Without the Navy and its global supremacy the Empire simply could not have happened, nor have been maintained and it is this centrality that gives the Navy its cultural significance as well. As Lawrence James put it in describing the global power of the Navy, and summing up what became known as 'gunboat diplomacy,' (which meant the Navy came and blasted you if you misbehaved):

> The Royal Navy can dominate every ocean – Gibraltar, Malta, Cape Colony, and later, Hong Kong. The Navy is a vital partner in trade. If you're a British businessman, shall we say, doing business in the Argentine, and your stock is seized by some local official, eventually the Navy will come to your assistance. So the Navy is a vital accessory to Britain's global trading. [6]

Or as another historian even more precisely said in respect of the thesis being advanced here,

> For a century and a half, from the Napoleonic Wars to World War II, the British Empire was the greatest power in the

world. At the core of that power was the Royal Navy, the greatest and most advanced naval force in the world. For decades, the distinctive nature, the power and the glory, of the empire and the Royal Navy shaped the character and provided the identity of the British nation. [7]

This was why the Battle of Trafalgar was so important, because it pretty much sealed Britain's complete dominance of the seas and Lord Nelson naturally became a national hero, and exemplar of British behaviour. In fact in a very recent opinion poll by ComRes for the United Kingdom National Defence Association [UKNDA] he was voted the all time great military figure. Nelson beat other famous British warriors such as Montgomery of Alamein and the Duke of Wellington to be hailed as the nation's best-loved military leader. Like other great British figures he has been immortalized through an endless re-telling of his heroism, and particularly the Christ-like death to which he succumbed at the moment of victory.[8] Why is Lord Nelson so regularly seen as a national hero and as the embodiment of British values? Both because of the importance of the Navy in the British story and because of the fact that he has been kept in the public eye ever since Trafalgar. Here's how Timothy Jenks put it, reviewing a new swathe of books about the great man

Books on Horatio Nelson appear so regularly that Britain's greatest naval hero hardly needed the commemorative assist of the 200th anniversary of Trafalgar to advance his bibliographical standing. [9]

In other words the business of defining who is a national hero and how they keep their place is an active, on-going process that governments, media and historians work at constantly. Every school child is taught the story of Nelson and almost every adult in the country will have drunk in a pub called the Lord Nelson, thus completing a virtuous British circle. In Our Island Story by H.E. Marshal she recounts the poem 'Rice' which so precisely spells out the ideas and emotions that surround Nelson.

Twas in Trafalgar's Bay
We saw the Frenchmen lay,
Each heart was bounding then;
We scorned the foreign yoke,
Our ships were British oak,
And hearts of oak our men.

Our Nelson marked them on the wave,
Three cheers our gallant seamen gave,
Nor thought of home or beauty.
Along the line the signal ran—
England expects that every man
This day will do his duty.

It is interesting to note how often poetry was the medium in which ideas of Britishness were expressed, a medium best suited to mythological and abstract ideas, and a medium not bound by fact or history. The romance of the sea, the heroism of the sailors and the glory of Britain are endlessly celebrated in all forms of literature, painting, prints and music, however.[10]

The mystical and mythological associations in the mind of the British between Royalty, Navy and Empire were discussed by Margarette Lincoln in her important book *Representing the Royal Navy: British Sea Power 1750–1815* in which she analyzes the social world of the Navy and its relationship to British society in general. It considers the cultural significance of the Navy in the period 1750–1815 by looking at key groups' attitudes to and relationship with the Navy in every sphere, from politics to the family. She is interested in how officers thought about and represented the Navy, and therein lies the core of the mythical patterns developed around seamanship, Britshness and moral superiority. She also looks at the important links between the Navy and politics, and how many individual naval officers entered the House of Commons in particular as MPs. Importantly she also looks at how the Navy and 'trade' got on, in other words how merchants saw the Navy, and the support which they provided. Empire, trade and war were the triumvirate that sat at the right hand of the Monarchy, and merchants and Monarchs whilst publicly deriding each other mutually supported the Navy as the modus operandi of the whole enterprise.

In some respects both the Army and the Navy throughout the history of the Empire projected the idea of unity and communality of purpose, a sharing of a burden that was of a higher importance than regional and local identity, and particularly over-rode ideas about class. National mythologies are regularly transmitted through the armed services as the embodiment of the greater will and 'the thin red line' or the 'British Tommy' was an important element of the gluing together of a nationalist story. The patrician elite at the helm developed a highly effective propaganda machine for the glorification of military valour, and the costumes and parades to accompany it. This was shown in the glorious uniforms concocted by the officer class in the Napoleonic era, and recorded in the portraits and woodcuts of the time. As Linda Colley puts it, 'Uniforms were the embodiment of authority, but they also denoted service to the nation'.[11] Elaborate, colourful (and expensive) uniforms were clearly not practical for the battlefield but were important to distinguish the elite from the lower orders:

'they served to distinguish members of the British elite from the rest of the population'.[12] Once again hierarchy is all-important whilst cleverly being combined with an idea that everyone was in it together, although this idea was often not seriously believed in by the proles, at least not all the time. The Navy was oddly enough seen as more liberal than the Army in the popular view, whereas the powers of Navy captains were actually greater than that of Army officers and they could flog, hang or do whatever they liked to the lower orders. In ruling the waves the Navy also ruled the way that the class relations of power were negotiated. At the widest level the other great symbolic connection in the mythology of the British Empire was that between the monarchy and the Navy, first outlined by Henry VIII and cemented by Elizabeth I. Or as Black puts it,

At the symbolic level, the fate of the Royal Navy was long bound up with the reputation of the royal family. This was seen in the review of the fleet at Spithead by Elizabeth II on June 15, 1953, in connection with her coronation.[13]

In the widest sense Britain's self-image about being a sea-faring nation derives from this centrality of the importance of sea-power and focuses on heroes, battles, naval-values and the romance of the sea, elements all found in fiction, painting, histories, stories and the reality of mass employment in shipping and the armed services. The Monarchy naturally became the symbolic focus of the British Empire and Queen Victoria's coronation as the Empress of India in 1877 was the high point of the Empire's global dominance, and interestingly was conceived by the wily Disraeli in order to deal with the endemic corruption of the East India Company and the growing disaffection of the Indian population. It was a hugely successful move both in India and at home, although of course it only postponed the inevitable; the independence of India. The duty of civilizing the Indians went hand in hand with huge payments to the officials, wealth being a natural concomitant of higher moral purpose and taxing the unbelievably poor Indian peasantry a necessity of raising them up to a higher level. No one has yet successfully explained the mechanism whereby making poor people pay taxes to rich people improves their life condition, but there is undoubtedly a proper reasoning somewhere. As Lawrence James puts it whilst discussing the endemic corruption In India and some attempts to reform it,

Efforts to cleanse the administration which, among other things, tolerated torture as a means of extracting taxes, were regarded skeptically by many In Briton who felt that there was something disturbingly un-English about the Indian Empire. [14]

The ennobling of Queen Victoria was precisely a political move to shore up British influence which had been severely damaged by the rapacious and outrageous behavior of the East India company, which possessed its own machinery of government and used it to plunder India in an extraordinary manner. Some historians apparently have great difficulty in deciding whether extracting money from an occupied country is morally reprehensible or not, but then these historians are probably the same people who aren't sure whether British involvement in the slave trade was a bad thing. Once again the ideology of the 'white man's burden' comes in very handy when discussing capturing and torturing people of another 'race' – and then selling them. If, as the British aristocracy always asserted, they were genetically superior then they did have the moral right to treat others as lesser beings, which was exactly what Social Darwinism argued, and in which they fervently believed.

This is where the great British virtue of hypocrisy comes into its own; self-delusion becomes self-fulfilling, and watching the lower orders starve to death in their millions, as they did in India and Ireland, is simply a natural process which can't be condemned, or interfered with, it is simply God's will. The greater hypocrisy of the British Empire was that whilst 'liberalism' flourished in the home country authoritarianism flourished in the colonies and a whole nation became deluded with its superior status; it is that delusion that Britishness is still confronting. The white working classes were taught that they too were superior, by virtue of their race, and again this delusion ended up defining much of post-war politics and led to Powell's absurd 'rivers of blood' speech and the rise of the British National Party.

The basic point about British identity is that the process of building the Empire, of controlling the seas and the dominions that were taken made it necessary to have a portmanteau identity, a combined character of those who served, be they Scottish, Irish, Welsh or English. This is the peculiarity of the British, it was an almost wholly invented identity, cobbled together out of Protestantism, Naval traditions, aristocratic rights and privileges and later Unionism and Social Darwinism. Practicality, pragmatism and a great deal of self-regarding mysticism went a long way, but it had to be worked at and constantly refined; that was the white man's burden. Keeping a myth turning over in the face of endless battles and contradictions is serious work.

Imperial propaganda in the nineteenth and early twentieth century was concerted, comprehensive and very successful, as every school history book, magazine and newspaper demonstrated.[15] The link that developed between ideas of Britishness, racial superiority and benevolent Imperialism are core issues in the ideology of Empire which were cemented by Social Darwinism in the nineteenth century. In his important work *Propaganda and Empire* John MacKenzie makes clear the racial character of Imperial propaganda as a consequence of nineteenth century Social Darwinism. The idea of the survival of the fittest was adapted through eugenics to give a 'scientific' basis to the idea of white superiority, which fitted very nicely with an Empire based on racial grounds. The importance of maintaining white superiority was always paramount, and highly regulated, the separation of the races was necessary to maintain the ideological basis of British rule. This tradition persisted even after World War II, states Mackenzie, since 'many of the popular attitudes towards Empire were [already] deeply embedded.'[16] That these ideas are core to historical British identity is another one of those tectonic problems that grind away below the surface of national heritage and nostalgia. You can take the colonies out of the Empire but you can't take the Empire out of the colonisers.

To reinforce and reiterate the historical truth of what the Empire was for, and how the British ran it, there is nobody better than the great colonialist himself, Joseph Chamberlain, Colonial Secretary, who, in a speech in 1879 pretty much summed things up.

> *We began to be, and we ultimately became a great imperial power in the eighteenth century, but, during the greater part of that time, the colonies were regarded, not only by us, but by every European power that possessed them, as possessions valuable in proportion to the pecuniary advantage which they brought to the mother country, which, under that order of ideas, was, not truly a mother at all, but appeared rather in the light of a grasping and absentee landlord desiring to take from his tenants the utmost rents*

he could exact. The colonies were valued and maintained because it was thought that they would be a source of profit – of direct profit – to the mother country. [17]

Later in expounding how the Empire should become civilised, and despite the bloodshed, he argued that there was a moral purpose to the enterprise, and that was in transmitting civilisation to occupied territories:

In carrying out this work of civilisation we are fulfilling what I believe to be our national mission, and we are finding scope for the exercise of those faculties and qualities which have made of us a great and governing race. I do not say that our success has been perfect in every case, I do not say that all methods have been beyond reproach; but I do say that in almost every instance in which the rule of the Queen has been established and the great Pax Britannica has been enforced, there has come with it the greater security to life and property, and a material improvement in the condition of the bulk of the population. No doubt, in the first instance, when these conquests have been made, there has been bloodshed, there has been loss of life among the native populations, loss of still more precious lives among those who have been sent out to bring these countries into some kind of disciplined order, but it must be remembered that that is the condition of the mission we have to fulfil.

This is precisely the ideology of Imperialism, based in a notion of British Identity as racially, culturally and morally superior. The combination of piety, pomp and the accepted necessary use of violence in order to further the aims of the British Empire gives a clear definition of Britishness that is, ultimately, racist and self-reflexive, as well as self-delusional. That is the legacy of the British Empire for the British people and it is that historical contradiction that cannot, but has to be, faced. The legacy of the British Empire is actually exceedingly grim, almost every territory that was once ruled by the British has been left in the twentieth century with endless political and civic problems. These range from failed statehood, political division and civil war stemming from what were cobbled together compromises that don't work, and the postcolonial effects of racism and hatred. The entire Middle-East, Iraq, Iran, Palestine, India, Pakistan, Bangeldesh, Burma, South Africa, Zimbabwe, Kenya, Ireland and Australia only to mention the most obvious examples; the idea that Britain gracefully divested itself of its Empire leaving a reasonable balance of growth and problems is a bit like saying that Genghis Khan introduced polo to the world as his legacy.

You cannot live in the past on the basis of ignoring the truth of power, racism and violence in order to celebrate how the home front was happy. Imperial Alzheimer's may be convenient but other people have long memories, and the consequences of the British Empire are still being played out all around the world. Historians battle over this reality all the time, and there are constant calls to celebrate the Empire and its achievements. The Prince of Wales convened a conference on the matter in 2003 to press for more traditional teaching to restore the story of the Empire:

More than three decades since the last pink-tinged maps of the colonies were hauled down from classroom walls across Britain, the empire looks like striking back. [18]

Leading historians addressing the Prince of Wales summer school for English and History specialists this week argued

*that Britain's imperial past has been ignored for too long,
and should be reinstated at the core of the secondary
school curriculum.* [19]

Professor Niall Ferguson, who recently presented Empire – How
Britain Made the Modern World on Channel 4, described the
subject as 'the big story of British history in the modern period'.
Teaching British history without it, he said, is like 'Hamlet without
the prince'.[20] Ferguson seems unaware that Hamlet is a made up
story and that, in any case, he was Danish and barking.

This fundamental problem of dealing with the legacy of the British
Empire is the Gordian knot at the heart of the identity issue and
is almost intractable, since it demands a national coming to
terms with a violent and traumatic past which is murky at best.
That convuloted amnesia is the generally accepted solution was
pointed out by Niall Ferguson at the conference.

*Ferguson accused university history departments, even
at Oxford where he taught until last year, of reacting to
national unease about the imperial legacy by deliberately
ignoring the subject.* [21]

In one sense dealing with the past is like psychoanalytic therapy,
you have to dig deep to confront the demons, and the resistance
to this activity is legendary, delusion and dream is infinitely
preferable.

Traditions have to be constantly re-invented and re-inforced and,
until fairly recently, it was something that the British were very
good at. The decline of Naval power since the Second World War
has gone hand in hand with a decline in the power of Imperial

ideology, despite constant attempts to revive feelings of tradition, and whilst not directly related there is a sense in which Navy and Empire have sunk together.

The argument that the British Empire was good for people can be considered in shorthand by thinking about India and Ireland and their histories in and out of the Empire. Ireland was ruled by the British with a rod of iron for at least 800 years and was the epitome of poverty, disease, forced emigration and backwardness. The brutality of the British in Ireland is now vaguely acknowledged, but it comes under the 'it was all a long time ago category'. The Irish eventually forced independence through armed struggle, and within sixty years became the Celtic Tiger, one of the fastest growing economies in the West with extremely high levels of education. The comparison is instructive.

Likewise India was ruled and civilized by the British for nearly 300 years and was backward, poverty stricken and disunited. After forcing out the British, who blithely divided up the area into unviable entities, India has turned itself within fifty years into one of the fastest growing economics in the world and a potential super-power. No doubt the apologists for Empire will claim that this just shows what we gave them in terms of civilization and a good start in life, the Mother nation helping give birth to healthy children. Or as the East India Company Report put it in 1812,

> *The importance of that immense empire to this country is rather to be estimated by the great annual addition it makes to the wealth and capital of the Kingdom.* [22]

The jewel in the Crown as India was known provided fortunes for the British throughout the years of British rule whilst Indian peasants died like flies in their millions, but we gave them railways and a civil service and cricket. In fact the East India Company which was established on New Year's Eve in 1600, was arguably the mother of the modern multi-national corporation. In an illustrious and unbelievably profitable career spanning almost three centuries, the Company bridged the mercantilist world of organized monopolies and the industrial age of corporations and was always only accountable to shareholders. This is exactly how the 'Empire' was actually a business enterprise that ensured a steady flow of capital back to Britain, where it was put to good use in driving the Industrial Revolution. India only officially became part of the British Empire in 1876 and before that was simply a semi-privatised trade zone where the Army and the Company mutually filled each other's pockets whilst praying loudly to the Christian God of righteousness. It was the separateness of the British from the 'other', the 'colonial' that was at the heart of everything in the Empire and it was this belief in absolute difference that allowed the hypocrisy of ruling, subjugating and exploiting to go hand in hand with the idea of civilizing. Funnily enough of course this superiority didn't stop endless Empire employees having discrete, and not so discrete, sexual liaisons with innumerable local women (and often marrying them albeit 'temporarily').[23]

Another interesting example of what the British Empire was about were the so-called Opium Wars with China in the 1840s. The East India Company was selling opium in China and bringing back tea but In 1800 the Chinese banned the importation of opium as its effects on users were severe. The British were not happy about this lucrative trade being blocked and in the war that followed, the Chinese could not match the technological and tactical superiority of the British forces. In 1842 China, at gunpoint, agreed to the provisions of the Treaty of Nanking, which were simply imposed.

Hong Kong was ceded to Great Britain, and other ports, including Canton, were opened to British residence and trade. By brute military force the British Empire forced a sovereign nation to accede to the importation of drugs for profit and to allow the British control of parts of China. The Navy bombardments of Chinese civilians were a key part of these drug wars, and once British control was established more fortunes were made selling drugs to the natives; however once again, some historians seem to have a problem with whether this was a good thing or not.[24] Another historian summed up these processes thus:

> The Opium Trade of the 18th century (which eventually led to the Opium Wars) when the Royal British Navy worked more or less hand in hand with the commercial interests of the East India Company, exemplified precisely such a link between war and trade. From the intertwining of war and trade, colonization was only a small step away. [25]

The British Empire had developed in a haphazard fashion over the years and took different forms as it spread and incorporated more and more territory, and different peoples; its complexity bred the need for order and for forms of domination that basically worked. Thus in one sense Britishness and race, as the idea of genetic superiority, were an almost inevitable development that gave a raison d'etre to the enterprise, based as it was in war, trade and domination. Social Darwinism was the theoretical ideology that reinforced the racial burden of the white man and gave final shape to the divisions and hierarchies of the Empire, which, as has been argued, was in some ways merely a greatly extended version of an aristocratic Navy's old and elitist traditions. The need to impose order from the centre, and the requirements of absolute violence in warfare conditions, meant that authority, and obedience, were key features of the far-flung Empire. Oddly enough the exercise of extreme violence often went hand in hand with endlessly flexible political tactics; whatever could be cobbled together and made to look Imperial, with a few uniforms and a bit of pageantry did the trick. This was the Genius of the British; but it had little to do with civilising and a great deal to do with trading, materials and money.

Britishness was similarly cobbled together with whatever poetic ideas could be dreamt up, borrowed or invented and was therefore an historically concocted set of ideas of natural superiority, innate character, divine purpose and a sense of duty and necessary privilige; which is the best of all worlds and of the British 'race'. The story of how these historical patterns also became a particular cultural, social, and psychological outlook will be considered later. Being British is still, in many ways, a state of mind, and poets, as has been mentioned earlier, rather than historians, have often been the ones who have worked at defining this peculiar state, as will be seen.

Chapter Four
In Love With Shakespeare

*'Now we sit through Shakespeare in order to recognize the
quotations.'*
Oscar Wilde.

When we think about these ideas of being British, and what
underpins them you keep coming back to certain key figures,
like William, sometimes known as the Bard and sometimes as
Francis Bacon, and sometimes as The Earl of Essex. Further down
the line there is Wordsworth, Byron, Tennyson, Kipling, Dickens
and all the other writers who so define ideas of Bitishness, but
Shakespeare is simply our national poet and the greatest Briton
ever, as well as officially the national genius. It may therefore come
as a surprise to some, if not all, that we don't really know who he
was, and whether he actually wrote the stuff. Whoever he was,
and whether the sonnets are addressed to boys or girls, he is, like
King Arthur, an absolutely central figure in the mediascape of the
British cultural assemblage. That it is very unclear who he really
was is very appropriate, since again the fact and the fiction are
so inter-twined that it is fundamentally impossible to say anything
with certainty, except that the plays and poems exist.[1] In one way
Shakespeare consciously helped define certain aspects of the

nascent Elizabethean political culture, and ideas about royalty, but he also unwittingly created many of the myths that we like to indulge ourselves with. Rather conveniently Shakespeare's birthday happens to fall on St George's day, so that the mythological can be pumped up all round. In Stratford-on-Avon they have the full-fledged birthday parade with mock Tudor actors, military bands, the police and bits of Empire regalia to reinforce the whole William-ness of us all. Shakespeare is our national poet and the embodiment of British greatness and any statement to the contrary is seen as basically treasonable, but who actually reads him these days? The Queen goes horse racing but I don't remember her turning up for matinees of Macbeth all the time, let alone with big Phil. School kids are forced to plough through Shakespeare and that generally puts them off for life. Funnily enough Karl Marx was a raving Shakespeare fan, and himself a failed poet, and the Russians adore him. Mrs Thatcher however simply thought she was Elizabeth, she didn't have time for the cultural stuff, except to insist British History and British values, as defined by her, were taught in school. So now in inner city schools kids who are refugees from Bosnia or Somalia are made to study this 400 year old poet as a means of discovering what life in Britain is like today.

As a schoolboy this author was told, and made to write down 'Shakespeare said what he meant, and meant what he said' something that neatly encapsulated an idea of William as the quintessential Brit, down to earth and clear. When confronted by the ambiguities and complexity of later Shakespeare that idea seems quite preposterous. [2]

Not once in ten years of study was it ever mentioned to pupils that there was a very serious question about the identity of Shakespeare, or that his politics might have been anything other than Protestant, royal and conformist; but since when did complexity, contradiction and truth ever come into education? Like Lord Nelson Shakespeare is kept alive by constant reinvention, histories, biographies, films, comics (manga Shakespeare is the latest thing) and even a work by the greatest honorary Briton, Bill Bryson. [3]

There is interestingly only one National Poet on the schools curriculum at the moment and he is, you guessed it, the Honourable William. He is, it seems, everywhere. Why is it that everybody is in love with the Bard at the moment, why is our national hero being given a make-over just for Hollywood, and why is everybody making films of or about William?[4] Alright, so he was voted personality of the millennium, whatever that means, but do we really need Shakespeare with our cornflakes as well as at the movies? What does his mythological status tell us about our self-regard and sense of Britishness? Did he spell out the core historical values of the British Empire? More importantly does he express the true beliefs and values by which people in Britain today live their lives? Does the twelve year old teenager on Facebook dig the iambic pentameters of all that complex courtly language?

Actually Shakespeare isn't as bad as he sounds, there is some very entertaining stuff in there amongst the rolling sweep of aristocratic persiflage that passes for speech in his plays. The really interesting question is why all the aristocracy of the media world are rolling out the Bard, or, as Barthes might have said, what does it all signify? Shakespeare is our National Myth, our signifier of all mythologies British, but why now? and why this tremulous insistence on our Great Poet, the speaking Icon of the sceptered Isle? One ventures to suggest that, rather like Serbia, when things are falling apart is precisely when the National myths are cranked out and wheeled around the shaky ramparts of the National culture. Repeating the mantra of Shakespearean certainty is rather like that faded Major character trying to call up the ghosts of cricket greens and honey for tea. It smacks of the quiet desperation that haunts the English as they attempt to ignore the collapsing marquees, the rotting institutions and the end of a low, deeply dishonest decade. There is, as William said, something rotten in the state of Notting Hill, or was it the Rocking North?

Obviously Shakespeare had a lot to say about mortgages, credit crunches and the nature of reality television; that is why we find him so relevant today. When the Serbs gather to rave about the battle of Kosovo in 1389 they look pretty silly, but when the British go on about Agincourt a soft cloud of miasmic hubris seeps across the media. Mediated through Shakespeare we can indulge our nostalgia to the full, and that is why he is so useful. There is a strange mythical conjoining of Arthurian, Shakespearian and Lord of the Rings type narratives that now even have junior off-shoot, Harry Potter, who brings them all into a jolly public school setting for teenagers.

Shakespeare is being rendered into an appropriately post-modern form for the Millennium and beyond, which means that he is being turned into a Hollywood pastiche that has them rolling in the Dome, and ready for the Olympics Yet why do we adore this figure, this man, this supposed playwright who was much ignored for centuries after his death? Or who really adores him, more importantly? That phrase about more in the breach than in the observance springs to mind here. He may be our official great poet and playwright but does he actually live and breathe in the culture we inhabit, or is he another figure in that great wax-works exhibition which is the 'official culture'. Here is a quote from a very recent Scottish cultural critic's blog.

A recent opinion poll indicated that 53% thought Shakespeare was overrated. An opinion poll conducted in my Scottish high school on January 16th 1988 returned a result that stunned the English Department and prompted a lot of shouting from the Masters. 100% of the student body thought Shakespeare was "total rubbish". [5]

In fact all students these days find Shakespeare difficult because he writes in an aristocratic language of 500 years ago, one that only highly educated elites would ever have understood, the idea that contemporary urban city kids will relate to it, or understand it, is akin to the idea that nobody likes drugs, or football. Here's an English teacher talking about the Bard.

I have huge problems with Shakespeare. You see, people don't like the stuff. They think he's boring. They find the plays and poetry really hard to understand. 'Shakespeare is rubbish' is something I heard from an adult two days ago and I'm used to hearing it from pupils. Teachers don't like teaching Shakespeare – just look at the staff room if you don't believe me. [6]

Perhaps everybody else is immersed in Shakespeare and goes to see his plays all the time but none of the students, nurses, lawyers, dustmen, call-centre workers or traffic wardens one comes across, or the post-modern riff-raff who go to local pubs and trendy wine bars seem to have any interest in this extremely dead white male, whoever he was. This is not a spurious attack on the Bard but simply reflecting contemporary reality in which ignoring him totally goes hand in hand with loving Shakespeare in a way that has become something like loving Diana, in other words a national emotional necessity. Have you noticed how often Shakespeare is quoted in the pub these days, how policeman always drop some witty quote from Falstaff as they nick you for speeding, or beat you up for failing to know quotes from The Tempest? Or how every time one orders a Mcdonald's they say 'Do you want a Sonnet with that, or is it a monologue to go?'

My local garage, run by a fat bloke and his son, won't let you leave unless you discuss the finer points of the Winter's Tale and whether Macbeth is nationalist or not! The driver of my Great Western Midland's train regularly intersperses his announcements about delays with jokes about 'Alls well that ends well', and references to Bottom, as do Ryanair staff and Easyjet. And as we all know, Shakespeare predicted the rise of the Internet and warned of global warming (The Tempest.) As all our other heroes crumble into the dust, the ancient and venerable figure of Shakespeare takes on a new and saintly light, and seems to personify all our glorious English/British characteristics, (if only he had played football as well). The fact that it's all a fairy story seems to matter not one whit, that he existed, and was probably more real than Jesus, or Arthur, stands him in good stead.

Wittgenstein, the Philosopher, famously said that the 'world is the totality of facts' and yet when it comes to The Unofficial God of Britishness there is hardly a fact in sight. All the evidence points to the immense probability that Shakespeare didn't write the plays, and that he was a front man for somebody else, or even a group of artists. It is no doubt deeply irrelevant to suggest that the real William Shakespeare was a bit of a roly-poly social climber with an abiding interest in food and money, but the scarce bits of evidence that there are suggest exactly that. The gilded youth presented in Shakespeare in Love more appertains to the Titanic than to the murky world of the Globe, and the dangerous world of Elizabethan politics and theatre. The Shakespeare Industry, what we might call the official British heritage myth, grinds on remorselessly however, and as the realities of the modern world appear ever more horrendous so the Bard becomes more friendly, as though he were turning into the Hobbit, only sexier. All the world may be a stage, but it is now an electronic stage in which simple myths, acted by very nice looking people, spread like a canopy across the privatized sky of our horizons. We all subscribe to the myth that the Bard is the best of British, that his genius still burns in every British heart, and that his plays are still deeply relevant to inner-city school kids, but we also believe that British cars are world-beaters. There is supposedly no other writer in the history of the world who is as relevant as he is, they would have us believe. Spain might have Don Quixiote but the British have the Bard. Myth, we might say, is the last refuge of the confused.

Just as a matter of historical interest here is a summary of William Shakespeare's actual beginnings in life quoted from the Oxford Shakespeare Society's website (which could mean anything).

He was born on the 23rd of April, 1564 of good farmer-class parents who could not read, could not write, could not sign their names.

At Stratford, a small back settlement which in that day was shabby and unclean, and densely illiterate. Of the nineteen important men charged with the government of the town, thirteen had to 'make their mark' in attesting important documents, because they could not write their names.

Of the first eighteen years of his life NOTHING is known. They are a blank. [7]

The site goes on to say that his letters show someone who is concerned with money, food debts and getting one over on his neighbours, 'he kept his genius so well hidden no-one at the time even vaguely remarked upon it. The vocabulary in his letters is nothing like the vocabulary in the plays and poems and show all the literary style of a country hick from Stratford, and his will just goes on about pennies and coppers.' [8]

The later part of his dynamic life runs like this:

1587 – he makes a ten-year visit to London, leaving the family behind.

Five blank years follow. During this period NOTHING HAPPENED TO HIM, as far as anybody actually knows.

Then – 1592 – there is mention of him as an actor.

Next year – 1593 – his name appears in the official list of players.[9]

The narrative continues 'Now aged thirty-three (practically average life expectancy at the time) nobody in the Universe had noticed anything about him that was worthy of comment, although his name was being associated with some plays.' He was still busy keeping his genius so well hidden not even his dog got a sniff of it. Then he continued his dazzling life by moving back to Stratford and in the words of the illustrious Oxford Shakespeare Society,

1610-11 – he returned to Stratford and settled down for good and all, and busied himself in lending money, trading in tithes, trading in land and houses; shirking a debt for forty-one shillings, borrowed by his wife during his long desertion of his family; suing debtors for shillings and coppers; being sued himself for shillings and coppers; and acting as confederate to a neighbour who tried to rob the town of its rights in a certain common, and did not succeed.

He lived five or six years – till 1616 – in the joy of these elevated pursuits. [10]

As many serious commentators have pointed out, this guy might have written all these plays and poems but, if he did, then why he spent his whole life pretending not to be able to, nobody knows. On the other hand rather a lot of the evidence points to the fact that someone else wrote them and he was the front man for various reasons, probably political.[11] Does all this matter when we have the great works themselves? Well yes it does, since believing in the genius of somebody as representative of our mutual and historical genius is somewhat affected by the fact that the guy wasn't who he said he was. It's like finding out that Santa Claus isn't real (not that we'd go that far here). The problem we are hinting at is that British myths unfortunately seem to fall apart when carefully considered, like St. George, Clive of India, Florence Nightingale, King Arthur, Robin Hood, Scott of the Antarctic, the charge of the Light Brigade, Margaret Thatcher, etc[12] (and, one might add, the idea of democracy) Not having a proper democratic constitution, just a mythical one is another of those strange little stories that is so British.

The pro-argument for William runs that the plays reveal great historical truths, endless wisdom and the most extraordinary vision of all humankind, as well as universal wisdom. Then it is argued that cultural studies may have deconstructed the plays to reveal some other dimension of structuralist wonder that Horatio missed, but we mere mortals are left with the plays themselves, and this is meant to be enough to carry us through into the twenty-first century. So what of the plays, how wonderfully relevant are they today? Quite frankly, apart from the one about boys like girls, one would have to say that they are about as relevant as Rudyard Kipling to understanding the multi-cultural, post-modern, technological utopia/nightmare that we now inhabit. If, like some upper-class cadavers that still infest some of our institutions, you believe in feudal responsibilities and being born to lead, then Shakespeare's historical plays are just the ticket, but for those of us who think the world has changed, they are creaking epiphanies to feudalism and reaction. What on earth children gain from ploughing through arcane and verbose verse, only to discover that what is being said is that all women are mad, dangerous or feeble, or beautiful but dangerous, escapes even cursory examination. As an over-educated Englishman of most modest means, one finds three hours of 'what ails thee my lord, when all the rooks do rattle in the arboretum' just a little bit predictable and dull, especially since the matter is often muttered. Put simply the style, the verse, the ideas and the language are utterly alien to almost everything we live today and anyone who argues otherwise is two computers short of a net-work. It doesn't matter how you dress the Bard up, he is a sixteenth century elitist who constantly implies that nobility is well, just noble, and the rest of us are no better than brothel-fodder. The Scots, Irish and Welsh are all quite comic as well just for good measure, along with the French, Italians and anyone else not from Tudory bits of the aristocracy.

The strangest claims about Shakespeare are that he is a democrat and a humanist, a man for all seasons and a lover of all, when clearly in all the plays he (the author) is a raving aristo-lover and a great hater of the common herd and the laughable plebs, whom he constantly portrays as drunken, smelly, stupid and so far below nobility that they occupy different universes. Is this really the kind of national myth we wish to perpetuate, the greatness of royalty and the idiocy of the herd? Actually quite a few people do, so perhaps that is the answer. The monarchist leanings in all the plays are there to be seen, and an implicit idea of class differentiation. Before anyone makes accusations of being anti-tradition let it be said that Chaucer has just a great a claim to being elevated to the national pantheon of all time greats, and he is even older than Willy-boy, and a lot funnier. Perhaps the difference is that Chaucer shows the great and the good as being nasty, selfish, vain and pompous, and ordinary people as often interesting, mocking and unimpressed by their Lord's and Masters. Strangely Chaucer also portrays women as sharp, funny, sexually active and quite liable to tip a piss-pot on the husband's head rather than swoon like a sylph or fall in love at the first sight of a Royal garter. Bring back Geoffrey should be the slogan, as well as Dickens, Hardy, Mary Barton, and Piers Plowman. Shakespeare may be the Jewel in the Crown, but like much else in Britain today the jewel turns out to be a fake, a glass bauble that convinces only those who want to believe. Would Shakespeare have a Royal company to his name if he'd constantly portrayed the upper echelons as being venal, corrupt, foolish and self-interested? It is definitely about 'As You Like it' and not 'All's well that ends well'.

Perhaps Shakespeare is the right hero for the currant phase since, after all, he was just a front-man for the real, aristocratic writer, and made plenty of money out of pretending to be something he wasn't (Celebrity ghost writer). Most of his plays mean practically nothing to most people but have a sort of mythical grandiosity which is like a signature tune; which is contemporary culture all over, 'a great deal of sound and fury signifying nothing' or in fact a brand name. Perhaps Land-Rover should think about bringing out a new Shakespeare car; it would have wood and leather all over it, go slowly and portentously, run over plebs without being asked, be very popular with tourists, cost a fortune and clog up all the entrances to theatres all around the country. Like the Globe and Inspector Morse it would make everybody feel better, perpetuate the mythology of British charm and carry on the tradition of avoiding reality which the British are so good at. It could be called an Aston-William and be driven in James Bond films. Jeremy Clarkson would love it and probably say that he had plenty of wellie, Beckham would buy one and so would rappers.

Somebody, most definitely not Shakespeare, wrote some very good sonnets once, but is that sufficient to erect a National culture on? Isn't there something rather oddly symbolic about teaching all our kids what we know to be a 'Great White Lie' and then all pretending that we adore endless dull performances of A Midsummer Night's Dream. In Shakespeare's Henry V there is that famous line which is used over and over again, when he is urging his men to fight on : 'God for Harry! England and St. George!' and it refers to the battle of Agincourt when the plucky British, vastly outnumbered, thrashed the villainous French and thereby set a standard which echoed down through the battles of Empire. Thus precisely is Shakespeare's propaganda value enshrined in a sound bite; poets have uses far beyond the aesthetic. The historical point is that the mythical status of Shakespeare goes far beyond his cultural value in a contemporary context, and his value to the Heritage industry is inestimable. His mythical vagueness is an asset in this business, he is all things to all men. Looking at the realities of Shakespeare simply brings into focus how constantly mythological the nature of Britishness is, and how heritage supplants analysis.

That the greatness of Shakespeare lies in his language is another claim, and this may be true, but it also reflects on the fact that the use, and misuse, of language is an important aspect of power. George Orwell often reflected on the nature of language and the peculiar ways in which it could be manipulated and it is this aspect of the mobilization of the Shakespeare myth that is interesting. In the emotional blending of poetry, myth and appeals to nationalism the stasis of the Great British Enterprise is constantly reinforced, and the beauty of Royalty exulted in the appeal to the hearts of all.

Shakespeare is wheeled out for all royal, and solemn, occasions and the Prince Harry brand is dutifilly employed to carry on the historical trends, the only trouble being that the contemporary Prince Harry precisely represents the ridiculous, out of date, absurdity of the whole enterprise. That he was discovered calling people 'Pakis' and 'Ragheads' comes as no surprise to anyone really because the Britsh aristo-thing really is that introverted, snobbish, racialised elitism that has no place in contemporary society. Shakespeare quite probably belongs in the same historical dustbin, except that poetry can always be revived; royalty, like racism. is past its sell by date.

Chapter Five
Class, Culture And Money

The distinctions separating the social classes are false, in the last analysis they rest on force.
Albert Einstein

Society in Shakespeare's time was highly stratified, the accident of birth defined the man, and so now of course we have completely left all that behind and Britain, apart from the royalty and the elite classes, is completely egalitarian. Perhaps in terms of access to parking tickets that is true but in most other things being born to the wrong parents is still a ticket to discrimination. Britain is without doubt one of the most unequal societies in the Western world but its self-image is one of democracy, freedom, fairness and dynamic contentment; on the Agatha Christie scale of strangeness this must place it top.[1] So why is inequality so little visible in the debates about Britishness? Historically the construction of the idea of Britishness rests on the way in which, as an identity, it overrides all other loyalties or realities of social existence thereby generating a cohesion of all peoples, united in values and outlook. This was the aim, and effect, of all Empire propaganda. The obvious question then, of course, is how far this idea reflects social and political reality. In other words how British are the British, and are all British truly British, or are some more British than others? Trying to understand how Britain works today involves these historical questions of equality, class, culture and power that have emerged ever more strongly in the twenty-first century, and those questions point squarely to the ways in which inequality still functions throughout the entire culture, with some modern multi-cultural twists thrown in. Most surveys about things British mention the Royal family, buses and beefeaters, and this abiding image and idea is highly significant, glossing over almost everything that exists in the real world. Mythology, in it's inimitable British variety, is what makes the world go round, closely followed by money.

In all the definitions of what constitutes Britishness, and particularly in external views of Britain, class, or the class system always gets a mention.[2] Naturally the official line is that all of that was in the past, the old landed aristocracy and the structures of deference have been replaced by a multi-cultural, classless society where the only distinctions are based on success and celebrity. Again, this is the official view of what makes Britain tick, we have left all that class stuff behind us and moved into this new, homogenous, ultra-friendly, multi-cultural nirvana. Then when people are asked what it means to be British they all say it means the past, the heritage, the unchanged way of doing things and the Royal family. One doesn't have to be an analytic philosopher to notice that there is something not quite consistent in the nature of this argument. To reformulate the question, it might go like this; 'In what way is a culture deeply embedded in its past but simultaneously no longer part of it?' This is very like the famous philosophical question of how dead is the deceased parrot, a little bit, just temporarily, or absolutely, totally completely dead? (This is parenthetically the deep existential question that lies behind the Monty Python parrot sketch, may God rest its soul.)

So as Jeeves might have said 'Yes, sir I percieve the problem.' Bertie might well have replied 'Yes, Jeeves we know the problem but what's the dashed answer? And hurry up man, I must whizz off to the club' The further question is what on earth explains the popularity of these class-ridden stories, and of the British love of class, deeply resonant of the aristocratic class structure on which the British Empire ran, and the snobbery that underpins them? Or the popularity of *Upstairs, Downstairs* or of *To the Manor Born*, or any of the other endless programmes that emphasise class, not forgetting *Steptoe and Son, Till Death Us do part, Keeping Up Appearances* and indeed *Coronation Street* and *East Enders*. As Sherlock Holmes might have said, 'Ahh, Doctor Watson, I detect a pattern here,' to which the eponymous Doctor would have replied, 'But Sir, as an educated Englishman of serious class status you'd obviously know better than the rest of us'. Speaking metaphorically the question is exactly why the British prefer stories and images over social and political change, and why the hidden truth of elitism and discrimination has been so easily reproduced and accepted by the culture as a whole? Or to put that more succinctly, class has been a central issue in British culture for a very long time, and, despite the contemporary flannel, continues to be so.

There is another mythology that basically runs as follows: sometime during the 1960s, helped along by rock n roll, we started to all hang out together and forget about how class defined how people behaved and prospered. This was accelerated by Thatcherism, which supposedly liberated everyone to earn money and own their own homes, and bingo, you had the classless society of the 90s and the totally classless society of Blairite Britain. Oxford was full of chavs and Eton mainly recruited scousers, and the pigs began flying everywhere, both literally and metaphorically. Arguing that class doesn't matter in Britain today is like arguing that a Morris

1000 is almost as fast as a Ferrari, or that being a Lord makes you intelligent. The real question is why does class persist so strongly, and why does the cultural inequality it breeds not go unchallenged despite being referred to again and again?[3] As Judith Cox, the journalist, put it recently:

> *British society today is characterised by a growing awareness of the widening gap between rich and poor. Outrage at the massive salaries and share option schemes awarded to those who run various industries has become a journalistic commonplace. But how do those at the top get away with it?'* [4]

Once more unto the breach and the breach is precisely the class divide; if we are all so tolerant and liberal and lovers of freedom, how come class inequality and discrimination is a) still so rife, b) so much ignored and c) so ensconced in the forms of aristocracy and royalty that still define the power structures amidst the endless chatter about British values. The short answer to this is that Britshness has always been a means of convincing everyone that we all belong together, and that we all have an equal stake in things continuing as they are. (The long answer is very complicated). That this ideological concoction has worked for so long is both tribute to its mythological efficacy and also to the stubbornness of working-class culture in Britain that doesn't want to transform itself. The British working classes seem to believe in the 'belongingness' of things more than anyone else, or at least as much as the upper classes. The recent backlash against immigrants is also to do with a white working class that feels it is owed a place in the sun and that others are taking it from them. The middle classes at the same time nurture their deep-seated dislike of the 'chavs' but keep it under wraps most of the time whilst quietly enjoying their access to education, culture, health services, money and privilege. The years since the 1960s have certainly seen changes, but they have mostly been in the nature of the middle classes, the nature of consumption and in the nature of the representation of class style in Britain. The fundamental divide about access to power, money, culture and influence has hardly shifted, and in some areas it has actually got worse in the last two decades.[5] As globalization has transformed the international labour market, the white working classes in Britain have got left further behind, but their commitment to the idea of 'our Britain' hardly seems to have shifted. This is a key question, why do people in Britain want things not to change, not to move out of the socially divisive patterns that have existed for so long and which, whilst providing psychological certainty, are so harmful to general well-being? What is this peculiar desire to live in a continuous past that, despite all the obvious massive changes, wants to feel that Britain is still the same as it has always been? The Countryside Alliance is another good example of this, having a rabid commitment to a form of 'country life' that has self-evidently disappeared, and which was never anything like their Archer's version of it. Fox-hunting is really the unthinkable in pursuit of the unalterable, hunting down the unbelievable. All the foxes, of course, have moved into the cities.

This powerful sense of continuity, of the fixedness of things culturally, of the impossibility of change, and its general undesirability, seems to be the glue that holds the class patterns in place in Britain. It is a kind of low-key stubbornness that is not absolute, but which, like donkeys on Blackpool beach, seems to have a profound grumpiness at its core, a cussedness that defies all rational explanation and which infects the lower middle classes just as much as the working classes, and in a different way, the upper classes. It is as though everyone knows Britain needs to change, and everyone talks about it a lot, but when it comes to it, like the donkeys, there is an almost absolute refusal to move, Northerners recycle jokes about the North, Scousers go on about their innate sense of humour, and Brummies moan about the fact that everyone characterises them as moaners. The upper classes get drunk and go shooting like some Monty Python sketch and complain about the bad behaviour of the lower classes, whilst the *Daily Mail* screeches about immigrants, just as it did in the 1930's. Somehow it is all completely different from the past, and bizarrely, it feels exactly the same, only the clothes, the cars and the food are slightly different. Everyone now wears Burberry and everyone indulges in road-rage, whilst listening to Jeremy Clarkson rant about the left-wing political correctness that infests the British National Party but the quiet hysteria of complaint is everywhere.

The Royal family are in the same houses (castles), the Old Etonians still behave like Old Etonians and the working classes do incredibly badly in education and mostly don't go to university, but they do buy lottery tickets and ex-council houses. Where the proles used to smell (according to Virginnia Woolf and George Orwell)[6] they now have fake sun-tans and go to Spain, and sometimes stay there. The middle classes buy places in France and Spain, go into the professions and worry about their pensions, whilst fleeing from the inner cities out into the suburbs. Everywhere class signals get very mixed but the morse code of distinction beeps quite loudly through the ring tones that echo round the streets. At every level of cultural expression, from football to opera, there is a concerted effort to change the class-based nature of audiences and activities, but apart from rich city types going to football not much has changed at all in the last hundred years. The arrival of media and celebrity culture has certainly changed perceptions of class and status but the underlying patterns of wealth and power have shifted remarkably little.[7] In fact working-class outcomes in terms of health, wealth and education are almost certainly worse now than they were forty years ago. The fact is that the media is less and less interested in stories about poverty and ill-health, they are mostly boring and do not sell papers. Celebrity, gossip, disclosure and stories about the romances of the upper classes are much better fodder for tabloids struggling in a multi-media market. Yet the facts remain that poverty, ill-health and lack of education are characteristics of the lower socio-economic classes. Recently a more extensive way of comparing poverty and wealth trends across Britain showed that inequality had reached levels not seen for over forty years. The gap between rich and poor has increased steadily, and the super-rich have more or less gone off the scale. This is according to research released (17 July 2007) by the Joseph Rowntree Foundation, who have conducted endless surveys that demonstrate the nature of inequality in Britain and which noble activity appears to have had hardly any impact at all.[8] In media culture inequality is boring and so pre the consumer boom, and the advent of reality TV.

So how much have things really changed since the 1950s when Britain first discovered prosperity for everyone, and the lower classes got bathrooms? Have class, wealth and life chances been dramatically altered, and is Britain now the home of complete social mobility? Is fairness spread across the land like Marmite on Hovis bread? As a recent commentator put it,

> In earlier times it was said of Britain's landed gentry that the first-born son took the title, the second went into the military and the third joined the church. So how much has changed? Look at Britain's royal family and the answer is: less than you think. [9]

This writer was referring to Princes Harry and William, but the overall picture still holds good. The Royal Family are the barometer of these things in many ways, exemplifying and exaggerating everything that is antiquated, unequal, ideological and peculiar in the British psyche. The contemporary Royal family are clearly rather dim, rather racist and completely unreconstructed in their attitudes to the world and to the lower orders, yet they are staggeringly popular. It was recently argued that the senior Royals weren't pleased about the lower-class origins of Kate Middleton, as her mother was, unbelievably, an air hostess. (Kate Middleton for those from Mars is a royal girlfriend) Her father was a pilot but really, she is not of the right blood, just to slip back into Empire thinking for two minutes, where U and non-U were such important considerations. Lord Lucan on the other hand, who was blue-blood to a tee, murdered people, listened to records of Hitler speeches all day and had fifty-odd similar suits, but he was loyal to his friends like a good chap.

Sir Anthony Blunt betrayed his country and lied about it for fifty years but this didn't preclude him from being Keeper of the Queen's pictures; perhaps that is a kind of community service for upper class types, a Royal ASBO.

Similarly the Diana story refracted the deeply peculiar psychological attachment the British people have to the idea of Royalty, and to moods of emotionality and gentle hysteria that are distinctly British, and distinctly maudlin. The oddly banal death of Princess Diana, in a drunken car accident, sparked the most peculiar wave of mass identification with the 'People's Princess' that it is possible to imagine. Sociologically speaking it seemed to be a moment of mourning that invoked all the loss and disaffection that the British were feeling about their entire culture, of Empire, of community, of family and of certainty in a rapidly changing world. This was a moment when the repressed hysteria that underpins the melancholic cultural memory of an entire people was allowed to be celebrated in public, and it was a shock to everyone, since no one recognised the symptoms of a depressed post-Imperial patient. Dysfunctional is the word that most aptly describes the media orgy that surrounded the Royal family after the death of Diana and led to masses of people lining the funeral route to weep about someone who was mostly a clothes model and charity glamour mum. What is particularly strange, and interesting, is that the masses turned on the older Royal family for their disdainful dismissal of the Princess of Pop who had caused them so much trouble, somehow articulating the oddly schizophrenic relationship that people actually have to class and power. Deferentiality co-exists with a seething discontent that erupts at the most peculiar moments in British society, thereby showing that hypocrisy is not the preserve solely of the political classes. This repressed dislike of the better-off, or of the Royals surfaces in many odd ways, and did so in the 1960s when the Royal family went through an unpopular period but recovered with some astute PR. Whether they will survive much longer is a more intriguing question

The interesting cultural point about class in Britain is that it is carefully woven into the fabric of the entire culture, so that those things that seem so quintessentially British, are tinged throughout with the feel and fabric of difference, which is presented as natural. *Brideshead Revisited* somehow encapsulates this perfectly, as does the National Heritage Society which is dedicated to worshipping old ancestral homes and upper-class lifestyles. The hymn to upper-class louche living that is *Brideshead Revisited* is also really a dreamy love affair with the past, and the British Empire, which is your average Briton's favourite fantasy; if you could bottle it the sky would be the limit. (another history porn version of it has just been made). This peculiar cultural dreaming is the product of the historical development of the British Empire and its attendant internalised classless sense of community, perfected into dream like states that are a combination of Hovis ads, *Coronation Street* and Red Arrow fly-pasts. The great British Empire was ramshackle abroad and a beautifully polished mythology at home; that was why class distinction in the shires could be bought off with the proceeds of racism overseas. This formula worked for three hundred years and underpins the racist laments of Enoch Powell's Rivers of Blood speech, an era of post-Imperial senility that was marked by Churchill's eventual demise and the embarrassments of the Suez debacle. This point was put like this by one historian, 'It is now well established' Woolacott writes, 'that colonialism has been an interconstitutive process that shaped British society and culture.'[10] In a colonialist society race is always a question and in this respect, culturally speaking, Alf Garnett was the last man looking back in anger.

The imaginary Britain that everyone occupied was ordered, like the Empire, was well run and everyone fitted in neatly, from Lord to Laird to peasant and prole. Whilst foreign money flowed in, and the army and Navy flowed out, there was work for most and a sense of fixity of purpose that suppressed most, if not all, discontent. The Home Front was this de-politicized space in which harmony was always seen as belonging in one's proper place, or to put that more simply, Britain was the peaceful centre from which the warriors sailed out to do battle with the world whilst the home fires were kept burning by the women. This global parody of home and Empire produced this quietly enclosed isle in which outsiders were seen as dangerous, deceitful, and like children that had to be disciplined. The class order of things, from Lord to factory worker, it was argued, was a fixed, fair and agreeable way of organising things so that everyone knew their place and was happy in it. This is the Toad of Toad Hall theory of British society, updated through many variations, the final version of which is Mr Cameron, posh-boy born to rule.

The lure of the gilded aristocrat, the power of imaginary superiority, is an extraordinary story in British history as over and over again upper-class lunatics have charged around the world causing mayhem, the Charge of the Light Brigade being the acme of such perfection. Suez being the final vanishing point when the whole world laughed at Anthony Eden, educated at Eton like his father and grand-father. His stupidity may not have come from Eton but his arrogance certainly did. This scenario of an incompetent elite mismanaging things has been wonderfully dissected by John O'Farrell in his aptly sub-titled book '2000 years of upper class idiots in charge'.[11] The story of the Queen's bank, Barings, and how it went bust as upper-class idiots cabled millions of pounds to Nick Leeson in Singapore because he said he was making billions is a contemporary version of the comedy of class superiority.[12] Hywel Williams' recent book on Britain's power elites also makes the point that 'social mobility is now lower in Britain than... in any other advanced country with the exception of the USA,' and cites figures to prove it. It is as though the sixties didn't happen, he argues, 'and that behind the casual informality that is now obligatory, the assumption of increasing classlessness has been decisively reversed.'[13] Despite all the media hype, celebrity culture and holidays in Spain the basic power structures have remained as they were, and that is the true illusion of classlessness. The question remains as to exactly why the British not only tolerate, but seem to enjoy, even wallow, in their subservience. Belonging is obviously an important psychological mechanism, but belonging to something that is injurious to your health and wealth would seem a bit contradictory. Some aristocrats might well argue, and some of them do, that anyone who puts up with the class system must self-evidently be not that bright and therefore, ipso-facto, of a lower class. Exactly what the sado-mashochistic tendencies of the British are in respect of how they fit themselves into strange cultural roles is a question that has been little reflected on but at some level seems to be a key question. Class belonging, and the iniquities of class culture, have arguably held Britain back throughout the twentieth century, as the inability to change and develop has led to a peculiarly static society. From the beginings of the Industrial Revolution, business, engineering and 'trade' have been sneered at by the landed gentry, and upper-class elites have mismanaged everything from industry, the armed forces, education, and latterly, banking. Wealth from the Empire has glossed over this for most of the time, and latterly North Sea oil, but the bankruptcy of Britain's culture is becoming ever more apparent. A society pickled in aspic can only survive in a cool climate, and the world is heating up at every level.

Class is probably best understood in Britain by thinking about language, and in particular the ways that English is used and spoken; historically it is the repository of the class psyche of the country. The very peculiar thing in Britain is that one's accent is very important in defining who one is, from street talk to posh, from Scouser to Brummie accent is everything. By comparison a sociologist noted that in Australia, which is forty times bigger than Britain, there is no such thing as a regional accent. Upper class, or received pronunciation, as what is spoken by her Majesty, has historically been taken as the benchmark of authority and was always used by the BBC and by Etonian Prime Ministers as they described the latest catastrophe to overwhelm the British economy. This Oxford, or Queen's English, marked the difference in class, particularly in relation to regional accents, on which the Empire rested. The snobbery of this class distinction was, and is, still a means of marking out difference, but it has become highly complicated because of inverse snobbery, which is a kind of class guilt found particularly in the middle class at University embarrassed by the realisation that everyone else is terribly middle-class as well. This was nicely summed up by Decca Aitkenhead in an article called 'Class Rules':

To be a middle class student just 20 years ago carried such social stigma that many graduates in their 40s recall faking a proletarian accent for their entire university education. [14]

This strange phenomena developed in the 1960s when, arguably, awareness of class privilege and of the historical burden of Britain's role in the world began to challenge the smug consensus of Little England, otherwise known as the Mother country. That was the era of the 'winds of change' when Africa achieved some freedom. The British Empire, the argument went, was sensibly and swiftly wound down and handed over to the deserving natives who had grown up sufficiently to warrant it. They had even learned to speak English and play cricket and we, as noble, paternal parents gave them back their countries, but funnily enough none of the money or assets. Class went underground in the 1960s and proletarian accents were everywhere, which aptly reflected the way the dominant culture changed its spots but kept its claws. Working-class people were still funny, as the popularity of Steptoe and Son and Till Death us do part demonstrated, but they could also be cool in certain circumstances as the swinging sixties brought fashion, photography and rock music into a new dynamic cultural sphere. The ruling classes hid out in their piles and went discreet, huddling together to worry about possible revolutions and the potential need for a military coup if Labour went too far.

Lord Hunt, the cabinet secretary of the day, discussed the plans that were made because certain sections of the Ruling classes thought Harold Wilson was a Soviet spy and likely to plot to introduce communism to Britain. In an interview Lord Hunt said,

> *I don't think they [the security services] were people who were in any sense evil. They were people who, on the whole, followed a train of thought that the Russians used to try and entrap everybody. They must have tried with him, [Wilson]. They must have succeeded.*

Lord William Waldegrave discussed the plots and the secret armies that were trained in this period and the idea of installing Lord Mountbatten at the head of a Junta,

> *Something had to be done. There were people talking about coup d'états. Lord Mountbatten was going to become head of some sort of junta that was going to rescue us, and so on. Where was this going to end?* [15]

This conviction of a class born to rule, and of the natural order of things, is deeply embedded in the British psyche and was brought out most strongly after the Second World War when the election of a Labour government seemed to many as the triumph of communism, rather than a democratic election, clearly won by labour. The fear and hysteria in the elite's consciousness was wonderfully spelt out by one Angela Thirkell in a series of highly popular novels in the 40s and 50s which charted the decline of the aristocracy and the rise of socialism(sic). With titles like *Love among the Ruins* (1948) it wasn't too difficult to follow her tone and in her novel *Private Enterprise* (1947) she discusses at length the terrible things that Bolshevik labour politicians might inflict on the struggling upper classes.

Angela Thirkell was an early Margaret Thatcher, and interestingly some of the rhetoric in Thirkell's novels emerges in the speeches of the Iron Lady, particularly in the echoes about lost greatness. Just as the literary had been so important in the construction of the idea of Britishness so it became a central place to mourn the passing of the greatness, and grace, of the aristocratic life of the Empire. Seemingly endless novels in post-war Britain lamented the passing of the old ways of doing things whilst a few, like Goerge Orwell and Patrick Hamilton mocked the fantasy of beautiful Britain and a harmonious society. Patrick Hamilton in *The Slaves of Solitude* savagely depicted the fading British in a novel that is as sociological as it is witty, set in a suburban boarding house it dissects the strange psyche of the British in the Second World War, and articulates the petty snobberies that plague British society. Rather than pulling together like in the movies, this motley bunch of snobs and fascist sympathisers tear each other apart. Nastiness and hypocrisy are articulated as British traits rather than the good manners of chaps in little moustaches, which probably explains why Hamilton's masterpiece went quickly out of print. Everywhere else however, from J.B. Priestley to Evelyn Waugh mainstream post-war novels lamented the falling morale of a nation that appeared to be losing its heritage and national prestige. There was a 'Building up Britain' government campaign in the 1950s but the contemporary novel was only concerned with the grey drabness that Labour governments and supposedly class politics were bringing to a war-battered Britain. Country houses were in danger and the masses were seen as on the march, and the ruling classes felt under attack. This paranoid theme runs throughout the latter half of the twentieth century and tells us a great deal about the supposed harmony of classless Britain.

From Churchill's attacks on strikers in the 1920s to Thatcher's denunciations of the 'traitors within' in the 80s Britishness only lasted as long as subservience was maintained. Britishness is about exclusivity and is constructed in such a way that it is an elite idea to which people aspire; Scots can just about be British but natives needn't apply, and the Irish are, as they say, beyond the Pale. Working-class people can be British but only if they talk funny, tug the fetlock and don't rock the boat, otherwise they are communist agitators.

So why does working-class culture appear so rarely in British literature, and why is it generally perceived as pathetic, generally funny and best kept below the stairs? Why have the working classes been so subservient over the centuries? The answer to this is that British ruling -class culture has always had the full weight of the Empire behind it, and the wealth and power to mobilize and contain dissent. From the 1680s onwards the job of Monarchy was to pull the Empire, and its people, in one direction employing pomp, pageantry and propaganda to do so. This was later aided by a massive popular press that was owned by types like Lords Rothermere, Beaverbrook and Northcliffe, who declared that he wanted to make the *Daily Mail* the 'paper of the British Army' and who controlled huge media empires dedicated to supporting the glorious Empire.[16] In the 1920s and 30s Beaverbrook and Rothermere suppoted a United Empire Party that was populist, jingoistic and put up candidates against the Tory Party, an interesting new line in press freedom and control. Basically from the 1850s onwards the *News of the World* has been peddling fun, sleaze and populist title-tattle to the masses, later joined by the *Mirror*, the *Daily Mail*, the *Express* and all the other popular papers that combine bingo, bonking, hysteria and commie-bashing as their main intellectual preoccupations. In this cultural development Britain was in the forefront and the creation of a 'mass culture' that Richard Hoggart so carefully analyzed in *The Uses of Literacy* and which Orwell discussed in his greatly underrated journalism, has much to do with the cultural and political quiescence of the proletariat.[17] Of course it is possible that the unemployed, under-educated and badly paid masses enjoy their place in the rain but on balance that seems unlikely. Buying off the proles with bread and circus, pomp and circumstance was really Britain's contribution to world culture and only in America's industrialised mass culture have we been surpassed.

The political quietism of the British working classes obviously owes a good deal to the Empire and its advantages, the buying into a psychological and cultural elitism that allowed a pride in the system and one's place in it. This political deal really only ended in the post-war era and it is its demise that Churchill and Powell articulated for the white working classes. Lenin famously came to London in the 1900s and looked disparagingly at the British Revolutionary movements and the Labour party saying

> *The Labour Party is a thoroughly bourgeois party, because, although made up of workers, it is led by reactionaries, and the worst kind of reactionaries at that, who act quite in the spirit of the bourgeoisie. It is an organisation of the bourgeoisie, which exists to systematically dupe the workers* [18]

Given what the contemporary Labour Party has just done for British workers this quote seems oddly apposite one hundred years later. (Mind you, they have accidentally nationalised the banks.)

When you consider the fact that working-class culture in Britain, with the possible exception of the Chartists in the 1840s and 50s, has been remarkably non-confrontational compared to its European counterparts, the cultural paranoia of the ruling classes seems quite bizarre. Conformity, consensus and patriotism co-exist with elitism, snobbery and class hatred, in both directions, producing a Britishness that is far more imaginary than real; that is what 'phlegmatic mysticism' means, the ability to indulge in a sentimental love of country that is simultaneously a dislike of much of what it constitutes, and if that sounds peculiar it is because that is exactly what Britishness is.

Class, Empire and culture are inextricably bound up in Britishness and the inability to move on from it is what holds Britain in such a bizarre cultural lockjaw. Brits hate going forward or going backward they prefer going round in circles whilst the music plays nostalgic songs. Here's another upper-class first class brain talking about the Empire,

If Imperialism means a certain racial superiority, suppression of political and economic freedom of other peoples, exploitation of resources of other countries for the benefit of the Imperialist countries then I say those are not characteristics of this country. [19]

It is odd how often people spell out the truth in an inadvertent, ironic way, and here Chamberlain excels himself in acutely advanced hypocrisy, the idea that Britain was there for noble reasons is exactly akin to George Bush's friendly invasion of Iraq.

Imperialism infests the soul and is a difficult drug to give up, as the Americans are currently discovering; giving up the historical memory is proving even harder for the British. This lingering of class, of position, of a tradition of ideas of importance is the British disease; combined with a dystopian tendency that hides not far below the surface it explains a good deal of the peculiarities of Britishness, and of why everyone drinks to try and forget what it is they have forgotten.

'The rise and fall of class in Britain should be the title of a musical, and of course 'The Ruling Classes' was a very good musical comedy, drawing on the honourable traditions of upper-class delusion, but this new musical would have a sour ending. It would be about how during the last twenty years or so, the widely accepted view that class structure and class analysis were no longer important grew up and also how it actually provides the key to understanding modern British history and modern British life. The opening song would be 'My Old Man's a City Banker' followed by, 'A Working Class Hero is Something To Be' which would lead into 'Everyone's a Princess for Twenty Minutes', with a chorus of 'Money, Money, Money' and the anthem of the current bust 'Home, sweet Home, she's gone away'. The closing chorus would be a group of ex-city workers singing 'The Death of a Chav' to the tune of 'Roll Out the Barrel.' Jade Goody would star in it and it would be sponsored by Endemol. The Royal family would watch it in secret and laugh as they played Monopoly with the Duke of Westminster. Meanwhile the white working classes (and others) in the North East will probably be engaged in race riots against immigrants from the old Empire, egged on by the very home grown British National Party. If Britishness is to be about fairness it may be time that ancient preoccupations, and power structures, were changed more in the real than in the wonderland of television and celebrity culture. The class distrust, antipathy and segregation that actually make the world go round may have to be confronted in real political reform, political will and the dismemberment of the structures of elitism that have been so carefully camouflaged by thirty years of pseudo-liberal celebrity culture. It may be time to have real democracy in Britain, to have only elected politicians and to dismember the absurd mock medieval pomp that passes for ceremony.

Chapter Six
The Great Hero's Chapter

*'Our tendency to create heroes rarely jibes with the reality
that most nontrivial problems require collective solutions.'*
Warren Bennis

Throughout the long history of the development of the British
Empire, and the attendant construction of Britishness, the
importance of heroes as role models has been highly significant.
Indeed in some respects the whole enterprise was heroic in its
aspirations, its scope and its grandeur; unfortunately, like all
heroics it covered up a multitude of everyday sins. From King
Arthur to Francis Drake, Captain Cook and Nelson and then later
heroes of the Empire, like Clive of India, Gordon of Khartoum,
Churchill himself, and all the other super-heroes of comic book
fame, the story of great men doing great things has been a vital
part of the building of a history. Despite the fact that Elizabeth I
was a woman, as indeed was the second Elizabeth, the heroes
of the great Imperial struggle were generally men, and of course
much of the whole business resounded around the entire idea
of being masculine, of being out there protecting the home, the
hearth and women. (That this sounds very like the Nazi *'Kirche,
Kueche, Kinder'* is no great accident in historical terms), the

ideological mission of creating a sanitised version of home, church and children is exactly the division of labour that went on with the organisation of the Empire and is found in all Imperial nations. Not only was the Empire hierarchical, it was also masculine in every way conceivable.

Heroes, like Gods, necessarily have to be masculine otherwise reality can get too complex, especially for the chaps. This is precisely why, if one takes a little time to consider it, the idea of Britishness Is really a thing that chaps do, and often to the accompaniment of smoking pipes. Women may be mothers, or occasionally like Florence Nightingale a nurse, but basically it was up to chaps to run around the world and conquer things in order to bring civilization to the world and trade and wealth back to Britain. King Arthur was the original, if completely fictitious, gentleman and British Empire heroes bestrode the world in similar Christian, patriarchal and very proper modes, as Winston Churchill recounted in his *History of the English Speaking Peoples*[1], which is a work that is, as people politely say, 'of its time'. In recounting all the great deeds of soldiers, sailors and explorers Churchill actually manages to ignore both the Industrial Revolution and women, the former probably being the single most important event in world history and the latter quite important too. This led Clement Atlee, Labour Prime Minister, to say of the work it should have been called 'Things in history that interested me.' It is said that Churchill probably took part in the last cavalry charge by the British Army and that resonance of old-fashioned heroism never really left him, nor his belief in Heroes, Kings and Queens and the British Empire. Schoolchildren were brought up on the Kings and Queens and heroes of British History, a narrative that included morality, duty, justice and service to the country and Empire.

This Churchillian narrative sustained Britishness probably for far longer than its natural life, and certainly into the post-war period when adapting to a new reality was a necessity, but proved psychologically almost impossible. The re-election of Churchill in 1951 was proof enough that nostalgia had already set in after just five years of a Labour government, and that his brand of heroics was like a drug to the British. This recurrent lapse into Empire nostalgia is still going on and the recent wave of historians defending once again the British Empire and all the great values of Biritishness is its contemporary manifestation. H.E. Marshall's absurd but entertaining book of heroics, Our Island Story, was recently re-published and became a best-seller all over again.[2] The revivalists even give free copies of the book to primary schools and it has been much praised in many quarters, only occasional voices pointing out that it should really be in the fiction category of the library. The Times Educational Supplement said, 'Our Island Story, first published in 1905, must rank as one of the most influential works of history of the 20th century.'[3] There is nothing wrong with telling children good stories but quite probably as adults historical truth should become a more important issue. Hero worshipping, like celebrity gazing, is a common activity in popular culture, but as the basis for a civilised society it leaves quite a lot to be desired and is really arrested development in psychological terms.

The innate British capacity to create myths and heroes, whilst claiming to be pragmatic and sensible, is quite wonderfully hypocritical in its delusional strength and seemingly inexhaustible continuity. The 'Back to the Empire' brigade exploit this weakness to the full. As one historian put it discussing Niall Ferguson's recent TV programmes on the British Empire,

> Ferguson is the Leni Riefenstahl of George Bush's new imperial order. Just as Riefenstahl's photography glorified

the violence of fascism and sold it to the middle classes,
Ferguson's Channel 4 series and book on the British empire
presents the acceptable face of imperial brutality. [4]

Arguing that the Empire was really not so bad after all, and the natives quite liked it too, has become something of a postmodern parlour game in the home counties, blithely defying all reason or historical accuracy. The battle about British history is clearly a deeply ideological culture war and despite the obvious fact that the world has changed dramatically, and that Britishness is necessarily being redefined, many of the old guard struggle on to defend the memory, the nostalgia for the good old days. Here's the Head of the Independent schools lobby at a conference:

Pupils should be drawing their heroes from British history
and not just the world of sport and pop music, says an
independent school head teachers' leader.

Edward Mitchell, chairman of the Society of Headmasters and Headmistresses of Independent Schools, says that pupils should be taught more about British history. This could mean giving young people the example of Churchill and Nelson, rather than Beckham and Eminem.[5]

In the annals of story telling about the British, Winston Churchill looms larger than life; his image and charisma are almost synonymous with the whole struggle of the British in the Second World War, his speeches are legendary and his bravery unquestioned. He summarised, synthesised and soliloquised on what it meant to be British and this creation of a character and of characteristics that were populist, powerful and propagandistic was an act of literary genius. His actual stewardship of the War, of the country and of the economy are different questions; we are here concerned with the mythology, the mysticism and the myopia that made up his reality in different ways. The story of the British people is the story that Churchill crafted in his journalism, his speeches and his books throughout his long and eventful political career, and it is now time for some re-evaluation of both. What is undeniable is that Churchill carefully made himself synonymous with a set of ideas about what it meant to be British, and did so in ways that owed a good deal to his journalistic background. In the Millennium poll of Great Britons Churchill came second to William, and that tells you a great deal. It tells you that many people fantasise about Shakespeare and culture, and that the self-made image of war hero that Churchill worked at so hard still resonates down the corridors of power and popular memory. In one sense Churchill is the last in a long line of writers, novelists, poets and painters who constructed the mythology of Britishness, and as a politician he was particularly well placed to forge the rhetoric on which it was based. That it was Imperialist, elitist and ultimately racist simply reflects the Victorian era from which he emerged and the Empire which he so loved. His career was a kind of permanent Dunkirk of the mind where he hung on against the odds and fought off all comers in defending his ideas, his position and the ideology on which it was based.

It is sobering to think that Churchill's early career was marked by constant changes, shifting allegiances and occasional disasters, nothing like the steadfast bulldog of later incarnations. His rhetoric of country, patriotism and democracy took him many years to hone, and it was only after the 'years of wilderness' that he found his audience, his time and his narrative voice. He was the great orator, the speech maker and the myth-maker, the man who fought them in the House, on the broadsheets and in the airwaves. He was Britain's finest haranguer, the man of the hour and the leader of a nation that needed to draw on all its mythological strength to mobilise the fighting spirit for one last battle. That war won, the battle for the legacy of the Empire, for the soul of the British and for a vision of a different Britain had to be fought, and in that his was the voice that weighed down the future with the endless lure of the past. Giving up the past, or even confronting it, has been Britain's Achilles heel and Churchill's contribution was to prolong almost forever that day of reckoning.[6]

Churchill's life story exemplifies everything about Britishness and the Empire, from his privileged upper-class background to his passionate belief in British superiority and the civilising role of Britain in the world. Born into the aristocracy at Bleinheim palace he had the normal public school education (Harrow) Sandhurst military academy followed by the army. With the right connections Churchill became an officer in the 4th Hussars and lived the life of the soldier/adventurer. Between 1895 and 1900 he saw combat in Cuba, India, the Sudan, and South Africa, experiences which he put to good use when he worked as a war correspondent and author. He was in every way an absolutely typical product of his narrow class background and his snobbery, ambition and Imperial outlook never wavered, nor his shrewd self promotion at every available opportunity. Such was his ambitious energy he was an MP for different parties and wrote for almost every pro-Imperialist paper in the land, so that, according to Lloyd George 'He would make a drum out of the skin of his own mother in order to sound his own praises.'[7] His mystical love of Empire and Royalty is so well known and rehearsed that it hardly needs adumbration, yet it is, on any analysis, extreme and overblown. Lloyd George also said of him 'He has no principles and no enthusiasm except egoism.'[8] One of Churchill's better lines in a discussion of his possible legacy was to say 'History will be kind to me as I intend to write it!' By sheer dint of will, perseverance and brilliant opportunism he did exactly that and those qualities, mixed with ruthless military judgement, led to his success. In the rhetoric of heroism he found his rightful place, and war gave him the opportunities he craved, much as the Empire had prospered in military adventure, force and the self-righteous subjugation of others. Churchill's genius was to translate the heroics of the Empire into a narrative of his own life, in which he was the greatest hero of all time, and this was a literary creation, a fiction like the Empire itself. The nostalgic glow that emanates from the Churchill persona after the Second World War is a combination of the historical record, the speeches and the brilliant propaganda that Winston employed at every turn, he was the spirit of Britain. So why did the electorate throw him out at the end of the war?

The gap between the high-blown rhetoric of Churchill and the grim reality of life in Britain is also a constant metaphor of the truth of Empire. It was an Empire of the elite and Britishness a confection of aristocratic ideals, crude nationalism and endless propaganda. Churchill's right wing Toryism and rabid anti-Bolshevism, which he saw everywhere, hardly endeared him to the nascent working-class movements in Britain, nor was typical of ordinary Britons. The poverty and ill-health of the lower orders was not something that concerned Winston and his opposition to unions was notorious. In fact Churchill had always been reviled by many, particularly the miners who he had attacked so often in the 1920s and 30s His disastrous leadership of the Dardanelles campaign in the First World War, which led to the deaths of 250,000 on the allied side alone, led to his resignation from Government and was not so easily forgotten by many. One author who was clearly not enamoured of him wrote:

With his lack of principles and scruples, Churchill was involved in one way or another in nearly every disaster that befell the 20th century. Winston Churchill must be ranked with Karl Marx, Woodrow Wilson, Vladimir Lenin, Adolf Hitler, Joseph Stalin, Herbert Hoover and Franklin Roosevelt as one of the destroyers of the values and greatness of Western civilization. [9]

There has been a good deal of recent re-appraisal of the Great Man's role in history and a good deal of it has been not terribly favourable, and it is interesting to note that even now such debate is met with fierce condemnation. It is a truth about heroes that they must be divine, they cannot have feet of clay nor imperfections, that is the point of them. It is because British History is so littered with heroes, and heroic deeds, that it is so difficult to deal with it, or to even recreate a more balanced story; criticism impugns the whole propagandistic edifice, which like Churchill, should not be touched.

This author can claim a world scoop here, as a thirteen-year-old schoolboy at a very old-fashioned Grammar school he ventured an opinion in a history lesson that Churchill was a 'war-mongering Imperialist' whose leadership left much to be desired. The elderly history master dragged the author out of the room by his ear, struck him round the head and awarded him two hours detention without remission. It was obvious to anyone that this was illiberal, reactionary and probably illegal behaviour but in the early 1960s this was the tenor of the times. (Perhaps Freudians would find motivations here.)

Churchill's death in 1965 brought about only the second state funeral for a non-royal (Lord Gordon of Kandahar being the first) and brought London to a stand-still as the country mourned the passing of the greatest living Briton, but the country he left behind was greatly changed and the Empire was gone. Britishness in all its Imperial glory and grandiose pretensions had been replaced by a country ill at ease with itself, economically backward, and seemingly in decline. The mass mourning was clearly at some level as much for the sense of loss of the heroic age, of the identity that had been recreated and rekindled by Churchill, of the age of heroism itself, for the very Britishness that mythology had been so mobilised to stage in endless pageants. His funeral, like his life, was a mixture of pomp, pageantry and propaganda, mixing naval symbolism, historical and military display and great use of the mass media, being watched on television by millions. This was truly the passing of a myth, the death of a hero and the last rite of the Empire ideology; it is little wonder that Britain came to a stop. The strange symbolism of the funeral barge and the echoes of King Arthur resonate throughout the service, allied to the Shakespearean grandiosity of the event to make this one of those performances that the British are so adept at.

Churchill was the last, and greatest, thoroughly British hero and actor. In representing British values he created a bravura performance that is constantly copied from the mode of speeches, the style, the down-to-earthness, the defiance, the quiet determination that is seen as such a British trait and the gentlemanly integrity and reserved Christianity. The true character of the impetuous, scheming and self-aggrandising opportunist is hidden in the smoke and mirrors of patriotism and emotional appeals to true Britishness. It is a miniature parody of the endless explorers and adventurers who built of the Empire such a glorious concatenation of private wealth and public splendour. Self-interest paraded as high-minded altruism, mixed with religious fervour and love of Royalty have always been essential attributes of British self-regard and Churchill has it in spades.

One of the truly great ironies about Churchill may well be, as several historians have argued, that his impetuous actions led to the demise of the Empire he so professed to be saving.[10] Churchill had been variously anti-semetic, anti-Bolshevist, anti-union and even, at one point, anti-American, something he quietly dropped in later life. He was convinced he was a military genius and constantly blamed, and bullied, other people when things went wrong, as they rather frequently did in his career. Another historian said of the great Saint,

> *One of Churchill's less attractive personality traits, aside from his refusal to accept the responsibility for the failure of his actions, was his ability to change his opinions at a moment's notice.* [11]

The evidence of his volatility and impetuousness is overwhelming, yet the myth still sates, and here is the Encarta Encyclopedia repeating it 'His true importance, however, rests on the fact that by sheer stubborn courage he led the British people... to victory'. Making speeches may well have helped morale but the people who did the actual fighting, and bore the brunt, actually threw him out of power when they were given the opportunity, perhaps recognising the difference between rhetoric and reality. Interestingly the armed services vote in the 1945 election which gave Churchill the heave-ho was delayed and unexpectedly was strongly pro-Labour, not perhaps the massive mythical support that history, or Churchill, awarded himself.[12] Incredulity was the word used to describe Tory reaction to the result and Churchill never really forgave the Labour party, or the Bolsheviks as he liked to call them.

Churchill then was a self-made British hero, a propagandist and class-warrior dedicated to preserving the rule of the Imperial upper classes to whom the entire world had been a playground for three hundred years. It is little wonder that he was unhappy to see it all slipping away, as it did in post-war Britain, which had lost an empire and failed to find a role or an excuse. That reality is still with us as Britain still struggles with the lure of the past, the opium of nostalgia, and the bitter truth of post-Imperial irrelevance. How then should the self-appointed hero be judged finally? Another recent biography summed it up fairly well:

> The aristocratic Churchill lamented the passing of the rule of his class and the growing influence of the lower orders; he was happy to pass measures helping them, but resented their demanding their "rights". His attitude towards the Indians was the same – with the addition of the racialism of his age and background. A man who distrusted democracy and wished to deny measures of self-government to India was not in tune with the spirit of the modern age. [13]

Historical truth has little purchase on mythological status however and in the common view Churchill is a great hero in the great British tradition and that is that. Just as the concept of Britishness is itself unquestionable in the minds of believers so the status of the demi-god Churchill is similarly non contestable. Britishness in this manifestation is basically a mode of religion in which rationality plays no part, and believing in Churchill is the same as believing in King Arthur, Robin Hood and Queen Victoria. Every country dreams in its own particular way but British dreams, because they are in black and white, are that much more convincing to the average Britain who, in any case, does not believe in dreams, only stories.

When Churchill wrote, or re-wrote, the history of the British he did it in such a way that all the complexity of regional, ethnic and class war was ignored and, most importantly, the vital history of scientific, technological and industrial development was hidden behind the pomp of warfare and coronations. What a bunch of upper-class lunatics did in a cavalry charge really does not compete with the transformations of society that were brought about by scientific analysis, technological insight and organised industrial production, without a Queen's Hussar in sight. As Harold Perkins observed, in his study of the development of modern British society

The Industrial Revolution was no mere sequence of changes in industrial techniques and production, but a social revolution with social causes as well as profound social effects. [14]

Part of the social revolution was the development of the working-classes in Britain, something that Churchill noted only insofar as they supported him, and when they did not he excoriated them as 'communists' and 'traitors'. It is a measure of the strange power of mythological thinking that even when he died in 1965 Churchill was still living in that Empire of the mind where heroism supplanted class and royalty smoothed over the schisms of political divide. Churchill's legacy, like the Empire's was a world of oddly shaped states, of colonial disaffections, of deep historical wounds and of conflicts that the British are still living through, not least in Iraq and Africa. Britishness in this context is a form of forgetfulness and denial of responsibility that is oddly characteristic of the man himself. Forgetting the Empire and absolving oneself of guilt whilst looking on the bright side and celebrating the past is a shorthand of the quintessential peculiarities of the British.

In a highly entertaining coda to this discussion of Churchill a recent researcher, Dr Richard Toye, a history lecturer at Cambridge University, has argued that Winston Churchill was a closet science fiction fan who borrowed the lines for one of his most famous speeches from HG Wells. He says that the phrase 'the gathering storm' – used by Churchill to describe the rise of Nazi Germany – had been written by H.G. Wells decades earlier in The War of the Worlds, which depicts an attack on Britain by Martians. Dr Toye also identified similarities between a speech Churchill made 100 years ago and Wells's book A Modern Utopia, published in 1905. 'It's a bit like Tony Blair borrowing phrases from Star Trek or Doctor Who,' Dr Toye said.[15] The element of spin and the recognition of a good phrase is a telling comparison of the two men, both self-conscious articulators of a publically created image and of a crafted persona.

In bringing Britishness up to date with heroes the gap between the assumed historical memory and the actual contemporary celebrity culture is a sharp divide, a reconstitution of image and belonging that poses difficult questions about what identity means. Culture today is mediated through the mass media, and particularly television and visual culture. Heroes are everywhere; from Beckham to Russell Brand and Cheryl Cole or Jade Goody they exist in a new dimension, where the everyday is heroic and shopping is the new frontier. In this brave new world the only Empire seems to be that of either star wars or Starbucks, and great heroes those who become A grade stars as opposed to military heroes. The strangeness of all this was mapped by social scientists recently in a poll of 3,000 teenagers about their reading habits and historical figures. Although not a large survey the results were interesting in showing what little actual historical grasp most youngsters had. For example one fifth of teens surveyed thought Sir Winston Churchill to be fictional, which in a strange sense he was. They also believed that Sherlock Holmes, King Arthur and Eleanor Rigby were real and more than a quarter (27 per cent) thought Florence Nightingale, the pioneering nurse was also a mythical figure. Conversely, a series of fictitious characters that have featured in British films and literature over the past few centuries were awarded real-life status, something that was discussed in previous chapters. King Arthur is the mythical figure most commonly mistaken for fact – almost two-thirds of teens (65 per cent) believe that he existed and led a round table of knights at Camelot. Sherlock Holmes, the doyen of detectives, was so convincingly portrayed in Sir Arthur Conan Doyle's novels, their film versions and television series, that 58 per cent of respondents believe. (as do many American visitors) that the sleuth really lived at 22b Baker Street An amazing 51 per cent of respondents believed that Robin Hood lived in Sherwood Forest, robbing the rich to give to the poor, while 47 per cent thought Eleanor Rigby was a real person rather than just a figure dreamt up by the Beatles. The study also showed a marked change in how people acquire their historical knowledge, not surprisingly now from the mass media. rather than books. Sadly, more than three-quarters of those polled (77 per cent) admitted they did not read history books, and 61 per cent said that they changed channels rather than watch historical programmes, suggesting that not even history mediated by television can engage the modern channel surfer for long. Paul Moreton, the channel head of UKTV Gold, which commissioned the poll, oddly argued that while there was no excuse for demoting real historical figures such as Churchill, the elevation of mythical figures to real life showed the impact good films could have in shaping the public consciousness.[16]

Heroes and Britishness may have had a close historical connection but it seems that we have ended not with a bang but with a Bond, Britain's best known hero of the last thirty years. Dreamt up by another upper-class utopian, idling his time away in colonial splendour in Jamaica, Fleming created the ultimate superior British agent, smooth, snobbish and ever ready to defend British values and effortlessly thrash the foreigner. We are back on the lawn with Francis Drake, heroically smoking before calmly dispensing with the enemy without breaking sweat, the only difference being that Bond smokes some exotic brand of cigarette rather than a pipe. Bond is self-consciously British, sauve, snobbish and committed to the defence of all things traditional, the all action hero who is also well-dressed. The popularity of the Bond films is part-super-hero and part nostalgia, but it is a formula that incorporates hundreds of years of heroes.

The fiction and the fact now seamlessly segue into the contemporary culture of Britishness and that is where the discussion has to go next.

Chapter Seven
The Lion And The Unicorn: The British Brand

Britishness is a complicated and enormous thing – what different people see as meaning different things. It can mean one island, a group of islands off the coast of Europe, or it can mean the British Empire – at times it means all those things. Politicians, and the rest of us, define it in different ways at different times.

David Cannadine, Historian

It is sublimely silly that on the British standard there is a lion and a Unicorn for it tells us everything we need to know about the idea of Britishness. The Lion refers to Britain's domination of Africa, the moral price of which is still being paid, and the Unicorn refers to the fantasy world that the British Lion occupies, a land of myth and nostalgic lunacy, not unrelated to the Land of Narnia. Indeed it is abundantly clear by now that Britishness is a historical construction, an imagined community as Benedict Anderson once put it, a cobbled together alliance of power, culture, money and Protestantism, which, combined with brutal global domination produced an Empire that spread across the globe.[1] The degree to which people identified with, or felt, British changed considerably in different historical periods, and it was probably most coherent in the Victorian era and during the first half of the twentieth century, not surprisingly since it was then that the British Empire was at its peak. Everyone at home benefited from the Empire, from lords to lavatory cleaners, because they all felt special about being the superior white man running the world; however the elite did rather better financially out of the whole thing, that was the point of the Empire. Trying to believe the British did things for the good of the natives, or for some higher Christian principle, is today rather like believing that smoking is beneficial or that footballers are sensible role models. The Empire was a semi-privatised global trading system which was transformed into a formal empire only in the later stages in order to solidify control, and the missionaries were the cheer leaders for a brand of superiority which was, literally, only 'skin deep'. Britishness was the brand name of the world's first truly global conglomerate, and its core values were white superiority, in culture and civilisation, but also in technology and warfare, and of course, naval dominance. Constructing Britishness as an identity was the formation of the home brand for the domestic market, incorporating the eccentricities of the Scottish, Welsh and Protestant Irish under the cultural thumb of the English. This brand is out of date.

Anti-catholic, anti-Irish, anti-black and anti-Semitic were pretty much core values as well, overlaid with a class snobbery and elitism that echoed from Eton to Edinburgh. The working classes were properly British when they waved flags for Royalty and communist agitators when they demanded decent living conditions. When the British died in their tens of thousands in the pointless First World War they were heroes, but when they got back to Blighty and looked for the land fit for heroes they found unemployment and economic depression. They also found Churchill making a political comeback by attacking the Bolshevik traitors in the Union movement who were fighting for a living wage; this from the hero who lived in a palace and drank champagne every single day. The historical truth is that being British was really about belonging to a club, but the rules were written by a secret committee that knew how things should be ordered, and by whom, and the masses were only ever allowed temporary membership.

The decline of Britain in the twentieth century is owing to the fact that, without an Empire to bolster its privileges the Club committee couldn't run a bowls club, or a railway service, or even a tombola draw, let alone an Empire or an economy. The other serious problem for Britain today is that the memory of the Empire doesn't just exist on the mainland but also in the cultures of those who were so professionally civilised by us. Whilst they may listen to the BBC in all corners of the globe, the long memories of colonial peoples may come back to haunt the British, particularly, one suspects, in certain Chinese quarters where financial might is becoming allied with political strength. Many of the immigrants who now live in Britain are of course from the Empire and the seeds of potential conflict and distrust are deep in the historical roots of all this.[2] Britishness may be trying to be an all-inclusive category in the twenty-first century but its past casts a long and doleful shadow over contemporary events, and whilst the British deny all responsibility for everything, many others have a different opinion.

Britishness as an identity is rooted in a whole series of delusions, mythologies and propagandistic stories developed around the Empire, many of which were designed specifically for the home front and which glorified and honoured the racist and exclusive ideas through which the Empire functioned. The correspondence of class snobbery and racist distinction fitted the Empire like a glove, and subtly kept the caste system functioning in Britain and India, as well as in Wales and Scotland, blithely supervised by the Anglo-German Monarchy who maintained the highest standards of aristocratic distinction on a global basis. The aloof, naturally superior British behaviour that was de rigueur around the world allowed the British to maintain an interesting distance from the clutter and chaos of the masses around them, silence always being a clever tactic of power. Part of the act was to appear distant and in control, another aspect of Britishness that is little remarked on. This demagogic act of psychological dominance, of crowd control, of appearing royal, of charisma is also something that British pageantry was well versed in. All these psychological dimensions are built into the self-regard of the British character, and remain in all the self-mythologising of the post-Imperial period. It may be said that the battle of Waterloo was won on the playing fields of Eton but in fact it may have been that the character of the British Empire was forged in the brutality and beating that went into the public school education of its upper-class cadres who were sent out to bully the rest of the world.[3]

In this respect Winston Churchill was the greatest Briton of them all in lionising the Empire, loving royalty and loathing the rebellious foreigners who endlessly plotted to bring down the Empire, but he arrived a little late in the day. Ironically, he bestrode the world in the Second World War only to find that the Americans undermined him in subtle, and not so subtle, ways leading to the inexorable decline of British power.[4] Churchill's entire career was really a kind of last rite for the Empire, and for the aristocratic ideals of Britishness that were the core of an elaborately constructed ideology. That he was re-elected as Prime Minister in the 1950s simply demonstrates how powerful was the hold of the Imperial fantasy in the minds of the British. In reality both were antiquated and feeble, not to say staggering into senility, and it was Enoch Powell who articulated this derangement in his claim that the white man was losing out and that the 'the black man will have the upper hand.' [5] this was the unconscious fear that has always haunted white supremacists. Powell was a ridiculous parody of a political leader and ended up where he belonged, with the Ulster Protestant crackpots who claimed to be truly British whilst sounding like nineteenth-century stalwarts of the British Empire. Powell is of course revered by the nice people in the contemporary British National Party and those right-wing conservatives who think we should never have let the Empire go.

Like other empires it could not last and, in reality, it had not lasted very long in its global form, but its impact on the British at home was as significant as its impact abroad. The long sunset of the Empire has been a painful experience for a people who believed both in their innate superiority and in their moral probity; the world does not seem too grateful for the legacy of Empire and, having lost an Empire, the British have failed to find a role in the modern world. The British brand of identity is still a powerful marketing tool but, as the ad men say, its core values aren't understood by the consumers, the British themselves. The fundamental problem is that the British, in fits of nostalgic amnesia, have expunged from their memory both the reality of global dominance, and of the means whereby it was achieved. This is an Empire of the Spotless Mind, where all bad things have been laid to rest and forgotten, forgiven and forever turned into quaint memories of living in India and lion hunting in Africa. Moving on is the slogan of those who want to forget.

The myth-making machine in Britain went into overdrive in the post-colonial period, developing the ideology of considered hand-over, of organised and sustainable withdrawal, as though it was planned and intended, rather than a long series of disorganised and forced evacuations of places that could no longer be held onto. It was probably Macmillan who started this peculiar process of pro-active Empire disbandment whereby in bowing to the inevitable Britain claimed that it had the moral high ground by giving back to people the countries that had been 'borrowed' or 'civilised' by the Empire for the sake of 'improving' the inhabitants. In this inimitable decolonisation, as in the handing over of India to the Indians in 1947, that great British exercise of haughty hypocrisy was manifested to the full. Stretched to the limit, and almost bankrupted by the Second World War Britain could hardly afford to keep the Empire going, or hold back the Nationalist movements in these countries, and blithely exited with as much dignity as could be mustered, which was considerable, if paper thin. Indeed it was another British invention to stage a glorious pageant of 'hand-over' in such a way that it mysteriously appeared as some deeply benevolent and purposeful act that was being conducted for the betterment of all, whilst masking retreat, disarray and an inability to properly allow for nation building. As India and Pakistan descended into mass killings and total disarray in 1947 the British congratulated themselves on a job well done, and Lord Mountbatten excused himself by arguing that it had to be done quickly.[6] Presumably since the British had only been there for 350 years the idea of what would happen after, or when, they left had never really come up, empire's are always so busy there is never time for thinking about things.

The Commonwealth was the wonderful solution to all of these conundrums whereby an undignified exit was made into a cheerful political solution that had all the hallmarks of a calm and sensible transition. It is this well-organised hand-over that is the basis of the British belief that it was all done properly and in the interests of freedom and democracy, and that moral duty was done in the best possible way. In fact the British Army was still killing people in Northern Ireland a few years ago, as in Aden, Kenya, Iraq, and all those other places that had complicated transitions to democracy. Britain ceded the political control of an empire in extraordinarily painful ways and then, in constant post traumatic stress syndrome mode, failed to come to terms with itself, the world, or the cultural truth of colonial dominance. For example parades were recently held in Northern Ireland to celebrate the return of the Royal Irish Regiment from Afghanistan, as they were in the 1850s, and the Protestant-Catholic sectarianism of the Empire days was still in evidence, as it is with every Orange parade in Northern Ireland itself. Ulster Unionism in its bizarre celebration of true loyalty to the Old Britain is a living reminder of how cultures resist realities and prefer entrenched ghetto status. One wag described the Orangemen as Protofarians, but the Orange Order's backwards looking attitudes could become embarrassing since currently Belfast is bidding to be a European 'city of culture' (whatever that means). Britishness in the twenty-first century may include art galleries for everyone but the pictures on the walls still have British landscapes in British colours, and in Northern Ireland they paint all the walls with Union jacks (except for the Catholic areas who disagree ever so slightly). Northern Ireland is a microcosm of the Empire and Bloody Sunday was one of the last rites of the British Empire., when protestant ascendency was enforced with extreme violence.

So where is Britishness today and has it moved into a bright new post-modern, multi-cultural, at ease with itself egalitarian place? According to Prince Charles, that doyen of modernity, it has gone into a hideous post-industrial time zone that includes horrible architecture, carbuncles and all sorts of things that are odious to the truly British way of doing things, Only in Britain could this ludicrous aristocrat make these sorts of complaints and get maximum media coverage, and be taken seriously, some of the time. He, and his ex-wife, Diana somehow reflect everything that is not quite right with the British, and the idea of Britishness, both in their ways of living and in their relationship to the real world of the ordinary British and the truth of nostalgic inertia. Royalty is a feudal idea based in eugenics and has as much relevance to the 21st century as witch doctors and shamans but it is still a central definer of Britishness. That there is virtually no discussion of this basic truth reflects a great deal about the weirdness of British culture.

However inasmuch as elitism, bizarreness and eccentric humour are meant to be part of Britishness, then Charles clearly is an important element, as is the long-running joke that his mother won't abdicate because she's worried that he'll alienate even the pro-royalty brigade once in the job. The dysfunctional Royal Family and the sheer absurdity of the very idea of royalty in the twenty-first century, are core factors in the inability of the British to become a properly grown-up country that deals with itself, its past and the realities of contemporary life. There is a profound political connection between inequality, elitism and hierarchical structures that is at the heart of the notion of royalty; as well as a deep contradiction about the idea of multiculturalism. That royalty and celebrity culture have combined to create a new form of hierarchy may look like a change in the right direction but in a strange way it is really just a new British Empire, the Empire of consumption, international money and the new world over-class. Lord Beckham and Lady Victoria now reign alongside Prince Charles and whoever the current wife is, but this is really a throw back to the glamorous High Society of the nineteenth century, with added new media glitz as the transitional ingredient. The educational, cultural and monetary gap between the rich and the poor in Britain is much as it always has been and in fact the very rich have become spectacularly wealthier during the last twenty years.[7] Short-term financial booms have certainly made everyone feel better off, and generally living standards have risen, but the actual divides between the bottom and the top of society have increased as the rich got richer. Trying to work out where all this has left the British is really a tricky question particularly since the gap between the real and the imaginary seems to increase with the general level of affluence in the country. The British addictions to heritage, nostalgia, distrust of foreigners and Europe, combined with anti-intellectualism, petty class snobbery and love of humouring themselves at their whimsical ways can only really be described as a mild form of psychosis. It is always said that people drink to forget and this may well explain the well known generalised drunkenness of the British, one of the few things that is truly classless. All of these tendencies are expressed in the slightly fanatical British love of the pound, our 'pound' and the refusal to join the euro, or take Europe seriously. That the pound may be about to sink under the waves as the good ship 'British Economy' crashes into the rocks is neither here nor there.

The very problematic question that all this raises is just what could Britishness mean if one took it all at its face value; freedom, democracy, fairness, sense of humour, love of heritage, tradition, good manners, creative, enterprising, artistic, multicultural and highly educated and successful and so on. If all these things were true then how come so many people also continuously bemoan the decline of Britain and Britishness? From Churchill onwards the refrain has been the decline of the country and the demise of all things British, indeed Thatcher made a whole career out of putting the Great back into Great Britain, which she supposedly did. We can trace this mood back to Britain's super power status at the end of the Second World War which at that time meant that it was taken for granted that Britain had a special role. It was assumed that Britain had special duties and responsibilities as a world policeman, a set of views that George Bernstein summarised as being:

> a description of the attitude to world affairs that all the main political parties shared in 1945. There was no admission of decline, even though there was a great deal of resentment that Britain had been forced to liquidate many of its overseas assets to save the free world. But the predominant feeling was pride. [8]

Losing the Empire has been an extraordinarily protracted process, which is still going on, and the delusion of Britain's special role in the world is still being played out in Iraq and Afghanistan. More importantly the Empire has come home in the shape of the bill for all that world domination, a bill which includes lack of investment in the industries and infrastructures of the home country, and the return of the natives coming to the mother country to find their place in the sun. All the British dominions were told that they were part of the Empire, of the Commonwealth of Men, and thus many of them exercised their right to visit, or live in, the beloved mother country, rather to the chagrin of the British here. Thus were the British hoist with their own petard. Britishness was supposed to be for everyone and here they were being that everyone, particularly when there were labour shortages that needed filling. The reaction to the decline of Britain's status in the world and to the change in the homogeneity of the population in Britain began to focus on 'foreigners' or immigrants, and the 1960s saw the beginnings of large-scale immigration from the Empire. Enoch Powell tried to whip up this nascent hysteria in his infamous interventions in Birmingham, articulating that deep rooted fear of the outsider, the 'negro' as he so intelligently put it. Using a peculiarly mock old-English voice he carefully spelt out the paranoia, the fear of change in the homeland, and the implicit claim of white superiority.

But while, to the immigrant, entry to this country was admission to privileges and opportunities eagerly sought, the impact upon the existing population was very different. For reasons which they could not comprehend, and in pursuance of a decision by default, on which they were never consulted, they found themselves made strangers in their own country. [9]

This claim of being made 'strangers in their own country' is the central articulation of resistance to all kinds of change, and particularly to multicultural change. The absolute refusal to recognise, or deal with, the legacy of Empire is compounded by the appeal to white homogeneity. Powell found much support from working-class groups in reaction to this speech and, famously, the London dockworkers came out on strike in support of him. He was sacked from the Cabinet, but his claim that it was like watching a nation 'busily engaging in heaping up its own funeral pyre' struck a note of deep resonance and has provided the benchmark for complaints about the decline of Britain ever since. Immigration, multiculturalism and integration have been the key themes of political debate during the last thirty years, and attempts have been made to redefine Britishness as incorporating these things, and with some success, but the deeply contradictory nature of Britishness refuses to go away. The contemporary white working class has been exercising to the full its right to wallow in the intemperate, and unjustified, racial dreams of another Britain where things were like they used to be.[10] The funny thing is that people talk about these contradictions a lot, but they roll on like rambling politicians in the House of Lords. Royalty, racism and reggae are a very strange mix.

It is not as though there isn't discussion there has been a legion of books about the state of Britain in the last decade, probably something in the order of 500 books across all of the areas of politics, class, history, culture, Royalty, the state of the economy and the general idea of Britishness.[11] These range from the academic, such as *There Ain't No Black in the Union jack* (1987), to Will Hutton's incisive economic analysis in *The State We're In* (1996), to the slightly morbid *The Death Of Britain*(1999), by Tory grandee John Redwood, and the very funny *Britain: What a State: A User's Guide to Life in the UK* by Ian Vince (2005) and the slightly dull and right-wing Contemporary Britain (2007) by Professor John McComick. All of them talk about the fact that something seems to be not quite right. In his *The Death of Christian Britain* (2000) Callum G. Brown looks at the central issue of the secularisation of Britain, something that many critics bemoan. George Monbiot looked at the business world's domination of Britain in his Captive State: The Corporate Takeover of Britain (2001) and, like Hutton, considered the neo-liberal impact of the long years of Thatcherism. The development of the gap between rich and poor was recently analysed by George Irwin in his Super Rich: The Rise of Inequality in Britain and the United States (2008) which demonstrated the continuing impact of Thatcherite deregulation. In the most recent phase the alarmist claims about decline and disaster have become ever more strident culminating in Melanie Philips' bizarre book Londonistan: How Britain Has Created a Terror State Within(2008). Many of these books centre on the idea that Britain has failed, politically and culturally, to adjust to the world after Empire, and clearly, there is a continuing problem about the British nation, and about the union of the United Kingdom. However, at the same time, there have been endless books that praise, glorify, or excuse the role of Britain in the world and demand that we return to the good old days, and the good old ways. Then there are books that claim that Britain is the nub of the new 'information economy' and the cutting edge of creativity and world finance. It's no wonder the average punter feels confused; the British in Britishness is either vibrant, rotting, or simply sleeping according to who you read. The present government has expended a lot of energy in trying to revive, to reinforce the values of Britishness, and it all seems a bit bureaucratic and slightly barmy. In particular the Citizenship test is one of the weirdest things on the planet, people are supposed to learn about Northerners eating fried Mars bars, and this will help integration? A citizenship test. complete with handbook, is a clear sign that the horse has bolted. This is the real nub of the matter, should Britishness be revived or should the life support system be turned off?

Basically Britain has been in a deeply conflicted state since 1945; the long-term legacy of Empire, aristocracy and Royalty has been a society in which deference, complacency and nostalgic cohesion more or less kept things in order; when the economic benefits of Empire receded, and the truth of long- term economic decline emerged, the idea of Britishness could no longer work. The last fifty years have been the slow and inexorable working out of this historical truth. The idea of Britishness is really rather like a leaky old Tudor galleon that takes in water through every seam, and it has needed the most desperate bailing out and constant hole-plugging to keep the creaky old thing afloat; and by taking on cheap foreign crew and throwing overboard a few cannons, along with the cook and the guidelines on how to sail. The white working-classes love all that old Tudor stuff almost as much as the Royals do, which is why they adored both everything that Powell the medieval ham said, and everything that Thatcher repeated as a sort of mock Churchillian back to the future. Every couple of steps forward, like sensible race relations legislation or abortion laws, were then countermanded by weirdly hysterical union bashing and reactionary legislation that tried to reinforce the ossified British state, endlessly post-phoning real change.

This one step forward, two steps back process has been the endemic political quadrille of British culture, where no one is actually brave enough to stop the dance and change the tune. Thatcher herself, the great revolutionary and reformer, simply shifted the political culture partly back to the Empire days where a bunch of privatising buccaneers pretended to do things for the state but lined their pockets at the expense of the people. Thus it was that her great invention of selling off council houses inaugurated the biggest organised plundering of public assets since Drake robbed the Spanish government in South America, and also led to the phenomena of house price booms and the currant tsunami of debt that is clearly going to overwhelm most of the country. Britishness as barmy consumerism dressed up as Victorian values must be the strangest and most unlikely economic policy ever thought of by even the weirdest neo-liberal neophyte in America. Having it both ways was ever the great traditional value of the British Empire; what Thatcher did was to modernise it totally by making de-regulated financial greed the same as good housekeeping. Unions were backward looking and dangerous but selling off the assets of the state in what was really a free-booting corporate raid on the accumulated wealth of the country was portrayed as a necessary return to the smaller state of the past. (The Victorians, oddly enough, established a lot of the state infrastructure). Thatcher's strange ranting, a mixture of imperious greatness and small town pettiness struck a powerful cord in the great British psyche and rather like a female Basil Fawlty she mixed insulting almost everyone with a bizarre appeal to everything that was wrong with the British. Her reforms of old-fashioned institutions only included those things that stood in the way of business enterprise and she effectively transformed Britain into the American model of deregulated capitalism wherein large corporations dominated almost everything. It is this unrestrained neo-liberalism that quite arguably led to the decline of most things that could be seen as British. So, like Churchill himself, the more she insisted on Britishness the more she undermined everything that it had historically stood for. Never, in the field of human politics, have so many talked so much and to so little effect.

In 1997 a Labour government was elected with a huge landslide and there was much jubilation in the shires at the demise of decades of Toryism and the promise of a better world, one in which a potential return to British values of fairness and decency was on the cards. Both Blair and Brown have talked about British values quite a bit over the years and, at the same time, again presided over the development of a managerial society run by corporations and which, in almost every respect, reflects American patterns of neo-liberal domination, which is the antithesis of a liberal Britain. Privatised prisons run by Group 4 and education systems run by multinational companies are so far from traditional British values that it seems perverse to carry on with the idea, but they do. Gordon Brown even argued in a speech in 2006 that Britain should have a day to celebrate its national identity, and set out to portray Labour as a modern patriotic party, whatever that is.[12] Brown declared it was all about 'progressive' ideas of liberty, fairness and responsibility, the latter perhaps explaining why Britain locks up so many people and why anti-terrorism legislation is about as draconian as it is possible to get in a civilised society. Orwell's notion of newspeak and double-think comes to mind in this context; when New Labour talks about progressive things it almost always entails some new managerial nonsense which limits everyone's freedom and gives control of everyday life to some global corporation which then screws the country for all it is worth. Thatcher's legacy to Britain is that almost everything, from trains and boats and planes to water, prisons, nuclear power and motorways are pretty much all owned by other countries, which seems a little strange for a country that prides itself on it's patriotism. Perhaps not owning anything allows Britons to be free, not having the responsibility for setting the price of gas or electricity or oil or any of those other boring details of everyday life. Not having a car industry, or almost any industry at all, also allows Britons to be free to get on with obsessing about house prices and football.

The British love of liberty, freedom and democratic rights, trumpeted from every quarter and in every myth about Britain, hardly stands up to any meaningful analysis. Indeed it is quite odd just how authoritarian and bizarrely bureaucratic the whole place has slowly but steadily become, all on the watch of a Labour government that sometimes pretends to be solemnly representative of the great British traditions. From the police to the prisons there has been a steady and dispiriting slide into what one columnist rather archly described as fascism-lite, which sounds ominous and captures the flavour of a deeply reactionary process dressed up in management speak and positive spin that makes locking up children sound like something from Enid Blyton. It is neatly captured in the horrendous and omni-present advertisements from the Benefits Agency that threaten 'We're closing in' and in darkly threatening text, warn that there is no escape. Then there are the ads that say 'We know where you live' which are everywhere. This is not the Gestapo but the television licence people, who seem determined to ensure that their Stasi image is fully justified. With their 'there is nowhere to hide' slogan the TLA scours the country looking for the evil criminals who watch television without having paid the licence fee. In hi-tech vans with massive databases at their fingertips these custodians of the BBC are ceaseless in their vigil to protect the rights of the government to produce drivel on television and force people to pay for it; and may God help those weirdos who actually don't have a television and refuse to conform. In all probability people should really pay the licence fee, but whether we need a massive force of seemingly deranged heavies who cruise the country day and night is another question. This may seem trivial but it is powerfully indicative of how a great British institution, the BBC, is now implicated in the constant erosion of freedom which it is historically supposed to defend. When George Orwell wrote *1984* he had been working at the BBC and he was aware of the authoritarian tendencies of the British government, as well as of the Communists in Russia. Were he around today one suspects he would detest the Blairite spin machine that Brown still uses on a daily basis, and the media that manifestly keeps the whole show on the road. Television in particular, whether in its reality mode or its populist mode, is also full of the double-think that pervades contemporary Britishness. Indeed, reality television allows the middle class entrepreneurs who run it to do their two favourite things; to make lashings of money and to take the mickey out of the ill-educated working classes whilst doing it. It's other function is to produce endless alarmist cops and robbers programmes that whip up the general hysteria about crime and violence whilst warning people 'not to have nightmares'; presumably as they cower behind the sofa at the insane levels of entertaining violence splashed across the screen.

The British idea of the Bobby on the Beat, which lingers like memories of tea on the lawn, is about as relevant to Britain today as cowboys on the range are to America. The police in Britain today are heavily armed, pseudo-military, seemingly completely divorced from everyday realities and highly enthused of all sorts of new technology, surveillance, new powers and expensive new cars in which to hurtle about behaving like American police in movies. This came to a head with the shooting of Juan Charles de Menedez in Stockwell tube, when a completely innocent person was gunned down by several undercover, armed police who had some vague notion that he was a terrorist, mainly because he looked a bit foreign. This terrifying incident, which is still being dragged through the interminable 'inquiry' process which the British have perfected over the years, brought home to many just how our civil liberties, the most basic of which is the right to life, have been eroded by the endless extension of state powers to combat terrorism (and television licence dodging). Ever since the 'New Labour' brigade took over this peculiar process of libertarian chat combined with Orwellian state surveillance and an increasingly armed police has become the standard fare of twenty-first century Britishness. Recently it has been announced that tens of thousands of police will now also be armed with Tasers, presumably so that drunken eleven year olds can be zapped without the police having to exert anything approaching physical effort or social control. This seemingly inexorable process of surveillance, management and new police powers has been going on relentlessly during the last twenty years and represents the truth of Britishness far more than the ideal of eccentricity and individualism. Brian Appleyard put it thus as long ago as 2001:

Privacy is dead. We are watched by 1.5m closed-circuit television cameras, more per head of population than any country on Earth. Our government, police and intelligence services have more legal powers to poke around in our private lives than those of communist China. [13]

Since 2001 the situation has got consistently worse, almost every aspect of life in Britain is watched, controlled, checked or spied on by legions of police, special branch, marketing analysts, hackers, social scientists, geeks, weirdos and local council officers. The problem is that as soon as you start talking about it you begin to sound like some nutter on the bus to Clapham who is just out for the weekend; it all sounds too crazy for words. Recently Phorm media in conjunction with BT carried out secret tests analysing what consumers did on the web so that advertisements could be targeted at them, and then expressed surprise that anyone thought there was a problem with it.[14] Parking wardens lurk in the streets in the middle of the night clamping people on yellow lines, and the Empire seems to come home here as well, when most of the wardens in London seem to be engaged in a spot of inter racial warfare known as parking enforcement.

Just to prove how peculiar it has all become Richard Thomas, the government's information minister, complained about increasing surveillance in 2006: and this from the people doing it. He was quoted as saying that fears that the UK would 'sleep-walk into a surveillance society' [15] have become a reality, which is a bit like a prison guard saying that locking up people isn't very nice. Apparently liberty and freedom are so British that they have to be monitored day and night. The report goes on to point out that

Researchers highlight "dataveillance", the use of credit

card, mobile phone and loyalty card information, and CCTV.
Monitoring of work rates, travel and telecommunications is
also rising. There are up to 4.2m CCTV cameras in Britain –
about one for every 14 people. [16]

Rather than being the home of freedom and the bastion of liberty that the myths propagate Britain is the worst country in Europe for snooping on its citizens and for infringing their liberties, as the Surveillance Society Report co-author puts it, saying

We really do have a society which is premised both on state
secrecy and the state not giving up its supposed right to
keep information under control while, at the same time,
wanting to know as much as it can about us. [17]

The endemic surveillance that characterises Britain was accelerated by the reactions to 9/11 and the decision to invade Iraq, followed by the London bombings and the massive reaction to those events. In the hysteria that followed these developments most of the civil liberties that Britons had assumed for hundreds of years were brought under threat, and damaged by the actions of governments that always put control and management over the interests of individuals. Briton has sleep-walked from the land of freedom into the twilight zone of bureaucratic insanity whilst waving the flag and reciting the mantra of Britons never, ever shall be slaves. They may not be slaves but they are controlled, monitored, watched and fined in ways that George Orwell would have had nightmares about in Room 101. In the land of the asbo the one-eyed camera is king of everything. The most recent discussions are about government intentions which, according to the Information Comissioner himself are that

There are plans to deploy 'black boxes' in UK ISPs'
networking hubs so that the government can capture and
record every website that UK citizens visit. [18]

This paranoid, controlling society is so far from the idea of a 'free' Britain, the land of the freedom-loving individual, whose home is his castle; that there is clearly a parallel universe in which the two co-exist. It would seem that with every new camera that is installed it becomes compulsory to proclaim that cameras are the very basis of traditional British liberalism, and that without them no one can feel safe. What all this suggests is that British society is really fracturing, and that the supposed values that hold it together went out with the advent of modern policing. Reporting crime is now done online, and presumably you get loyalty points if you constantly report things, and of course crime rates are falling faster than the leaves from trees with Dutch elm disease.

The decline of Britishness is really about the decline of traditional communities, a process that in one sense is always going on, but this time it really is about the passing of ways of life that had evolved slowly over many decades of continuous development. The basis of community, a shared set of values, has been steadily undermined by the political, commercial and managerial revolution that has transformed Britain from an averagely incompetent nation into a high-tech, very rich and alienated society in which consumerism and conflict have replaced local patterns of behaviour. Every aspect of contemporary life in Britain is difficult, anonymised, commercial and business driven and geared to maximising money-making at all levels of society. Christianity has been replaced by entrepreneuralism as a mode of religion and this has occurred without anyone really noticing, although the Church of England has actually commented that most churches are empty. Fundamentally the neo-liberal model of advanced capitalism inaugurated by the blessed Margaret and reinforced by the shiny New Labour lot has destroyed anything that could pass for old-fashioned Britishness.

This may sound like an extreme claim but it is really an accurate description of what motivates most people in Britain today. TV programmes like the *Dragon's Den* are much more reflective of British society than is the Archbishop of Canterbury. The insane financial boom of the last ten years has simply reinforced the British addiction to credit, spending, consumerism, foreign holidays and the religion of house prices, which is clearly now going to be a long and painful lesson for people in debt management. The new Britain is technology obsessed, mobile phone addicted, and deeply prone to loving reality television and scandal about stars and Wags. A few Guardian-reading oldies go to Hay on Wye every year and pay homage to Saint Alan Bennett, laureate of the eccentric deceased, but they are the thinking classes who think that class stops you thinking. There is nothing quite so British as the polite disdain of the educated classes for their uncivilised brethren from the suburbs and council estates, those to whom being called Chantelle is improbably endearing. The bolshieness of the lower orders is actually refreshing, despite it deriving from the strange anti-intellectualism and anti-education patterns that have also persisted in the dream of Britishness. Everyone, of whatever class background, seems to be united in the constant refusal to acknowledge that the world is very different or that in fact everyone's behaviour has changed unimaginably. The Queen may have worn flares and the entire British economy gone up in smoke but the old-fashioned dance still has to go on. In fact *Strictly Come Dancing* seems to be a profound metaphor for the contemporary zeitgeist; as the world goes up in flames the British are obsessed with some portly old geezer dancing very badly in a mock reality TV programme. He is quite British, quite eccentric and quite entertaining, and of course went to Cambridge and is deeply middle class, so that's fine. That he used to be a political reporter also sums up many things about the contemporary world: politics in a real sense is far less important than nostalgia, entertainment and television. Probably the next reality TV show should be something like *'Gardening on the Titanic'*, or *'I'm an economist get me out of here'*.

The final question is this. Can the bizarrely idiosyncratic cultural formation that passes itself off as a coherent organic reality, otherwise known as Britishness, actually survive and be a useful model for conducting affairs in the twenty first century when the whole world has changed, the environment has collapsed and the ways that people actually think about the world have been seriously undermined by the reality of the collapse of capitalism. We can summarise in this way. Are Prince Charles and his lovely wife Camilla the real role models that young Britons aspire to in 2009? The fact that it is even a question says a good deal about the very peculiar place that is Britain, and suggests that the catching up that needs to go on is almost equivalent to the entire stock of mythical stories that stretch from King Arthur to the BBC decision to sack people for being rude on prime time television. Put this another way the British are addicted to stories, in a way that is really quite juvenile and psychologically peculiar. It is as though Dickens and Hardy, along with Mr Kipling, who make very fine stories, have infested the British psyche with a narrative virus that makes them susceptible to any kind of story, as long as it has a good ending. The strange popularity, still, of Enid Blyton and Agatha Christie add weight to this thesis, the British cannot divest themselves of rampant story-telling. Perhaps this is why British culture and literature are so creative and energetic, and why the media and music are all so successful, it all goes back to the nursery and to the 'Once upon a time' in which Peter Pan was so proficient. It just seems that in the Twenty first century it might be time to pull back the curtains and to take a hard look in the broad daylight at the very strange place that Britain has turned into. From royalty to *Shameless* there are connections, and common pursuit of an amnesia that is mindful more of Miss Havisham than of modern life. Here in the twenty first century it might be time to move into the twentieth.

Post-Script
Last Night of the Dogs – August 16th 2008
Walthamstow Stadium

After 75 years of dog racing at Walthamstow stadium, (the 'Stow'), a wonderfully idiosyncratic, thirties-style building that looks as if it should be at the sea side, the owners called it a day as the punters were no longer showing up. The stadium has been sold to property developers and will be pulled down, ending up as new homes and a supermarket. Going to the Last Night of the Dogs felt very much like a Goodbye To All That occasion, and sharply illustrated how traditional British things have evolved and changed. When the stadium opened in 1933 dog racing was a popular working-class sport and everyone went in the 1950's White City stadium used to host 100,000 at evening meetings and there were 30 tracks in London. Amy Johnson, the aviator, was at the opening night at Walthamstow, which was the smartest new stadium in Britain and played host to film stars and traditional East End Gangsters like the Krays. Even Churchill gave a speech there in the 1945 election, which apparently didn't go down too well. All in all it was home to a traditional East London culture that was firmly rooted in working-class attitudes and pleasures. Its closure reflects just how much things have changed over the last thirty years, and nothing reflects it more precisely than the appeal by David Beckham to keep it open.

Oddly enough his first job was at the track, collecting glasses for a minimum wage, before he became a mega-celebrity, international star and multi millionaire. The irony is that as a working-class boy from East London he would no longer be seen dead at such an unglamorous place; the world, and celebrity culture, have moved on, only the rest of us are going to the dogs.

There is a 'Save our Stow' movement that is having some effect, but clearly over the last twenty years dog-racing has declined spectacularly, as have many other traditional activities, including going to the pub and having a 'knees-up'. British culture, once supposedly centred around the pub, has gone global, digital, interactive and computer based, just like the rest of the world, and pubs close at the rate of three per day in Greater London. Despite its iconic status, the chances of saving 'the Stow' are very remote and it is really only the strength of nostalgia that has produced any reaction at all. One punter described the stadium on the last night as 'like St Paul's, the Tate Modern and the Science Museum – an iconic part of London,' thus says Claire Walker, who is visiting with her husband, seven-year-old daughter, niece and nephew.[1] Everyone talks about the loss to the community and the decline of traditional culture, which is clearly true, but nobody actually wants to go there and would rather go to Ibiza, whilst bemoaning the decline of tradition. This schizophrenia about cultural matters is exactly where this book started out. Here's another punter articulating precisely this emotion. 'Another part of white working class culture sent to the dustbin. Along with all the old fashioned pubs that are closing down, what will London look like in 20 years time? Full of Costa Coffee houses and identical rabbit hutch flats, with people running pubs that have about as much personality as a door handle, how boring!'[2] The ultimate irony in this nostalgia mode was probably Ronnie Kray opining that criminals in the old days were much more honourable than the dishonest types of the 1990s who attacked anyone, Ronnie commented that 'In our day we had respect and we only killed other crims, not just anyone.' Like Dixon of Dock Green and the Archers everything used to be in its place, very British and much better than today, which is why everybody wants to get away from it. Once again denial and nostalgia seem to be the key factors that influence the way Britons think about themselves.

So how was the Last Night at the Dogs, this paean to the past this celebration of the great traditions of working-class culture, this bacchanalian bun-fest of Britishness? Well it was pretty British, really. When you got to Walthamstow tube there were hand made signs everywhere that warned you that since it was the last night of the dogs there might be delays on the buses, despite the fact they had run for 75 years without a problem. When you got to the stadium there was a giant queue to get in which seemed to take for ever, despite this being the most advertised night at the dogs ever. Piling into the popular enclosure was fun, and at £3 has to be the cheapest night out anywhere but, because so many people had turned out for the last night, they had run out of programmes, vital to the whole experience. After clunking through the old-fashioned turn styles the place was abuzz, and especially the bar which, in traditional fashion was under-staffed and profoundly inefficient, then traditionally running out of beer. Some of the staff were Polish, which soon brought out a nice bit of loutish British racism as underage chaps with gelled up hair demanded pints and 'What the f*** is going on?' By eight o'clock only slightly warm light ale was available since management planning had clearly not extended to people turning up for the last night and wanting draught beer. Still, after you waited twenty minutes for a drink you really did enjoy it, and it should be said that the prices were distinctly reasonable.

The plastic mugs for the beer really gave it that up-market feel that went with the whole occasion. (The omens for the Olympics are all positive in this sphere.)

Without a race-card/programme it was difficult to tell what was happening, and the antiquated board with strange numbers on it didn't help, nor did the fact that the intercom sounded like Waterloo station on a particularly bad, foggy, damp and impenetrable day. There were queues for the Tote, queues for the loos and queues for the bar and even a queue to throw your money at the bookies, who, taciturn to the end, gleefully filled their bags. One 'geezer', stripped to the waste and sun-tanned stood at the top of the steps giving a running commentary on all the '******** twats' who were blocking the place up and not knowing what they doing; true to form he was complaining that outsiders had turned up and were spoiling the party. This was Britishness at its best. The main clock on the central information board didn't work and was stuck permanently at 9.20pm and then the traps themselves jammed for the last race but one. Still, it was all quite good-humoured, slightly sordid and deeply nostalgic; even the media was there recording the protest about closure and everyone jostled in the queue to get pissed and forget why it was we were all annoyed about something or other.

Post-Post Script

Walthamstow stadium closed, the underground closed intermittently, and then Woolworth's closed down as the great British bubble burst and the lunatic credit binge that had sustained the story about Britain being at the cutting edge of information technology all ground to a halt. This is a turning point in the endless story about Britain which will not have a happy ending and in which the unity of the United Kingdom, or Great Britain Plc as it is known, is coming under severe strain. Britishness is finally going to have to be looked at as the antiquated, past its sell-by date story that it really is. It will all be like telling kids that Santa Claus doesn't exist, and in fact was really a German invention anyway.

Britain leaves itself in denial, in mourning for its mythical past and completely unable to come to turns with the future. The currant financial disasters engulfing Britain are also related to this myopia in the sense that much of the blame for the insane bubble that was the housing market came out of a belief that Britian was different, and superior, and that we knew best whilst silly Europeans still clung to old-fashioned ideas about manufacturing and regulation. Brown wallowed in the fantasy of the great British boom, calling it sensible and sustained when it was no more than a giant out of control credit frenzy. The delusional aspects of all of this prove again that Britain is a nation addicted to mythical thinking, denial and phlegmatic mysticism. It is Up the British without a paddle, just a pipe-dream.

End Notes

Chapter One
What Is Britishness

[1] *The Telegraph* 17 December 2007.

[2] *Advanced History of England, Book VI* (1905). W & R Chambers LTD. London. p.279.

[3] *The Telegraph* debate. 18 March 2004.

[4] Hansard 19 May 1941.

[5] Ibid.

[6] 18 March 2004.

[7] A wonderful discussion of all this looking at the novels of the period is *After the War*(1993). Taylor, D.J. Chatto and Windus, 1993.

[8] Ibid. p.13.

[9] Mitford, Nancy. (1956) *Noblesse Oblige; An Enquiry into the Identifiable Characteristics of the English Aristocracy*. Hamish Hamilton.

[10] Ibid.

[11] Wright, Patrick. (1985) *On Living in an old country*. Verso books. p.5.

Chapter Two
The Stories We Tell Ourselves

[1] Stewart, C.A. (2008) *Very Unimportant Officer: Life and Death on the Somme and Passchendale*. Hodder, London. (There is a Ph.d to be written on the pipe in British literature).

2 Churchill undertook the production of a newspaper, a rag called The British Gazette, the sole aim of which was to spread propaganda lies that there was a drift back to work etc.

3 The Telegraph.co.uk 26 May 2008.

4 *Chambers advanced history of Britain, Book VI.* p.6.

5 BBC2 has just started yet another glossy period drama simply called *'The Tudors'*.

6 <www.heritage-history.com> 'Old-fashioned history straight from your great-grandparents bookshelf.' A very British website.

7 Levin, A. (1994) *King Arthur's Death in Legend, History and Literature*. A Thesis Submitted to the Faculty of Stevens Institute of Technology in partial fulfillment of the requirements for the degree of Bachelor of Arts.

8 Twain, M. *Acknowledgments for A Horse's Tale.*

9 Phlegmatic mysticism describes the peculiar disease that the British suffer from, it comes from constant exposure to stories and myth which develops into a fully-fledged inability to distinguish fantasy from political reality. Centuries of story telling increases the symptoms.

10 'Definng Britishness' Historical Critical Practice No 73. January 1987.

11 Colley, L. Britons. (1994) *Forging the Nation. 1707 – 1837*. Vintage, London. p.396.

Chapter Three
From Armada To Empire

1 James, Lawrence. (1998) *The Rise and fall of the British Empire*. London, Abacus, p.169.

2 See the important work Hobsbawm, E.J, (1992) *The Invention of tradition*. Cambridge University Press.

3 Osborne, Richard. *Ideas of Britishness*. Intervention. No 17. 1976.

4 Borsay, Peter. (2006) 'New approaches to social history. Myth, memory, and place: Monmouth and Bath 1750-1900'. *Journal of Social History,* 22 March.

5 Herman, Arthur. (2005) *To Rule the Waves: How the British Navy Shaped the Modern World*. Harper Perrenial.

6 James, Lawrene, op cit. p.163.

7 Black, Jeremy. (2005) *A Post-Imperial Power? Britain and the Royal Navy Orbis*. p.353.

8 7 August 2008 UKNDA press release.

[9] Humanities and Social Sciences Online. July 2006.

[10] Twas in Trafalger's Bay is also the name of a painting and there are many of Nelson, and naval triumphs, plus the films and comics ad infinitum.

[11] Colley, L. Britons. (2003) *Forging the Nation, 1707-1837.* Pimlico. p.199.

[12] Ibid.

[13] Op cit, Black. p.65.

[14] Op cit James, L. p.155.

[15] MacKenzie John M. (1984) *Propaganda and Empire. The Manipulation of British Public Opinion, 1880-1960.* Manchester University Press.

[16] Modern European History, Spring 1995, Professor Geoffrey Giles.

[17] This speech was delivered at the annual dinner of the Royal Colonial Institute on 31 March 1897.

[18] Nicholas Pyke *The Guardian.* 5 July 2003.

[19] Ibid.

[20] Ibid.

[21] Ibid.

[22] *Imperial Finance under the East India Company, 1762 –1859.* Duke University Press (1996).

[23] See chap. 6 in Paxman, J. (1998) *The English: A portrait of a People.*

[24] The literature is extensive but see *Mo, Timothy An Insular Possession* (1986).

[25] Yi-Jia Chen. (2002) *The Opium Wars*, Kapiolani Community College. Horizons.

Chapter Four
In Love With Shakespeare

[1] See Bryson, B. (2005) *Shakespeare: The World As Stage.* Atlas/HarperCollins.

[2] It is often pointed out that many plays were co-written and ideas taken from all over the place, making clarity almost the last possibility.

[3] Re-issued as *Shakespeare: The World as a Stage (Eminent Lives).* Harper Perrinial (2008).

[4] There are a minimum of 300 films that have been made based on or about Shakespeare – ten in the last five years. See <http://www.insidefilm.com/

shakespeare.html>.

[5] See Red Room, <http://www.redroom.com/blog/alan-black/shakespeare-overrated-english-rubbish>.

[6] English teaching Online. <http://www.teachit.co.uk/custom_content/newsletters/newsletter_aug05.asp>.

[7] Oxford Shakespeare Society. <http://www.shakespeare-oxford.com/?p=119>.

[8] Ibid.

[9] Ibid.

[10] Ibid.

[11] See Michell, J.F. (1999) *Who Wrote Shakespeare?* Thames & Hudson.

[12] See Lytton Strachey. (1969) *Eminent Victorians.* Harvest books.

Chapter Five
Class, Culture And Money

[1] A report by the Office for National Statistics (ONS) contains damning evidence of the growth of social inequality in Britain over the last few decades. Aptly titled 'Social Inequalities', the report compares indices from the end of the 1970s up to April 1998.

[2] British Council survey, September 2006.

[3] New labour constantly talk about it ending poverty, challenging discrimination and equal access to education.

[4] <http://pubs.socialistreviewindex.org.uk/isj69/cox.htm> The Illusion of equality is undermined by the facts. The wealth gap under labour has actually increased in the last decade.

[5] Over the last decade, wealth and power in Britain have been consolidated in a tiny new class at the top. Michael Meacher, MP. guardian.co.uk, 20 June 2008.

[6] Orwell says this quite often particularly in The Road to Wigan Pier and Virginnia Woolf comments on it in her diaries, after the one time she met some proles.

[7] Sampson, Anthony. (2004) *Who Runs This Place? The Anatomy of Britain in the 21st Century.*

[8] See the Joseph Rowntree Foundation website for their extensive research into this question.

[9] Alan Cowell, 7 September 2003.

[10] Woollacott, A. (2001) *To Try Her Fortune in London: Australian Women,*

Colonialism, and Modernity.

[11] O'Farrell, J. (2008) *An Utterly Impartial History of Britain: (or 2000 Years of Upper Class Idiots in Charge).* London, Black Swan.

[12] Denton, N & Gapper, J. (1997) *All That Glitters: Fall of Barings.* Penguin.

[13] Williams, H. (2006) *Britain's Power Elites: The rebirth of the ruling class.* London, Constable and Robinson.

[14] Class Rules. (2007) *The Guardian.* 20 October.

[15] Talbot, Ann. (2006) *Britain: Documentary reveals plan for coup against Wilson Labour government—Part 1.* 19 April.

[16] For Example See Thomson, J.L. (2000) *Politicians, The Press And Propaganda: Lord Northcliffe And The Great War, 1914-19.* Kent State Press, USA.

[17] Hoggart's analysis of the decline of traditional working-class culture has never been surpassed and Orwell's writings describe many aspects of the better sides of poverty in Britain.

[18] Lenin's Collected Works, Volume 31, pp.213-263.

[19] Neville Chamberlain, British Prime Minister. (1939) Quoted in The British Empire Is Worst Racket Yet Invented By Man, *New Leader,* 15 December.

Chapter Six
The Great Hero's Chapter

[1] Not completed until the 1950's these books are completely written in Churchillian mode, in other words the history of heroes.

[2] The Civitas/Galore Park project to re-publish Henrietta Marshall's classic children's history book *Our Island Story* has been supported by *The Daily Telegraph.*

[3] 7 July 2005. One hopes this is just wish fulfilment, and it is certainly grossly untrue.

[4] Jon E Wilson, Lecturer in History, King's College, London 8 February 2003 <http://hnn.us/comments/8301.html>.

[5] BBC. 10 March 2003.

[6] Emmet, K. (1989) *Winston S. Churchill on Empire.* Carolina Academic Press.

[7] Quoted in *The Political Beliefs of Winston Churchill* (1980). Addison, Paul.

[8] Ibid.

[9] *The Real Churchill,* by Adam Young, Ludwig von Mises Institute <www.misesorg>

This review appears in Finest Hour No. 123, Summer 2004, p.38.

10 Buchanan, P.J. (2008) *Churchill, Hitler and the Unnecessary War: How Britain Lost Its Empire and the West Lost the World.* Potter Style.

11 Hasring, B. Another view of a paper God. TBR News. 19 April 2006.

12 Childs, D. (2001) *Britain since 1945.* 'Churchill's defeat'.

13 John Charmley, Professor of history at the University of East Anglia. 29 January 2005, *The Independent.* From *Churchill: The End of Glory; A Political Biography* (2004).

14 Perkins, H. *The Origins of Modern English Society,* 1780-1880 London, (1969).

15 By Sarah Cassidy, *The Guardian.* 27 November 2006.

16 Aislinn Simpson, *The Telegraph.* 4 September, 2008.

Chapter Seven
The Lion And The Unicorn: The British Brand

1 Anderson, B. (1991) *Imagined Communities; Reflections on the Origin and Spread of Nationalism.* Verso.

2 In Turkey last year the papers ran a big spread about a very old guy who came forward and claimed he had been raped by Lawrence of Arabia in the 1920s and this was given national prominence. Memory is clearly long lasting in many places, not just Britain.

3 Immortalised in Lindsey Anderson's classic film 'If' set in a typical public school.

4 Roosevelt famously arranged meetings with Stalin that excluded Churchill in 1943/4.

5 Powell, E. Speech in Birmingham. 20 April 1968.

6 This is the standard excuse for the inter-ethnic massacres that occurred, no-one apparently could have predicted them and it all happened so suddenly. See 'Mountbatten Messed up Partition of India' Syed Arif Hussaini, Pakistan Link, 14 July 2006.

7 See Hasseler, S. (2000) *The Super-Rich: The Unjust New World of Global Capitalism.* Palgrave Macmillan.

8 Roy Hattersley review of the Myth of Decline by George Bernstein. (2004) *The Guardian.* 10 April.

9 Enoch Powell's famous 'Rivers of Blood' speech, as delivered in Birmingham on 20 April 1968.

10 See Baggini, J. (2008) *Welcome to Everytown: A Journey into the English Mind.*

Granta books.

[11] For example there have been at least 25 books this year on Englishness or Britishness.

[12] Browns speech reported on the BBC Saturday 14th January 2006.

[13] 'No Hiding Place', Sunday Times Magazine. 15 April 2001.

[14] See ISP review for details of the trails in 2006/7.

[15] Surveillance Society Report, BBC 2nd November 2006.

[16] Ibid.

[17] Ibid.

[18] Ibid.

Post-Script
Last Night of the Dogs – August 16th 2008
Walthamstow Stadium

[1] Quoted in the *Evening Standard*. 19 August 2008.

[2] *Evening Standard*. 19 August 2008.

Further Reading

Advanced History of England. Chambers New Scheme Readers, Chambers, 1905.

Anderson, B. (1991) *Imagined Communities; Reflections on the Origin and Spread of Nationalism.* Verso.

Baggini, J. (2008) *Welcome to Everytown: A Journey into the English Mind.* Granta books.

Bernstein, George. *The Myth of Decline.*

Black, Jeremy. (2005) *A Post-Imperial Power? Britain and the Royal Navy.* Orbis.

Bradley, Ian. (2006) *Believing in Britain: The Spiritual Identity of 'Britishness'.* IB Tauris.

Bryson, B. (2005) *Shakespeare: The World as Stage.* Atlas/Harper Collins.

Candappa, Rohan. (2007) R*ules Britannia: The 101 Essential Questions of Britishness.* Ebury Press.

Colley, Linda. (1992) *Britons: Forging the Nation 1707-1837.* New Haven, CT.

Colls, Robert. (2002) *Identities of England.* Oxford.

Christpher, David. (2006) *British Culture: An Introduction.* Routledge.

Davies, Norman, (1999) *The Isles: A History.* London.

Fabian Society Review, Winter 2005: The Britishness Issue.

Gatrell, V. (2006) *City of Laughter: Sex and Satire in 18th Century London.* Atlantic Books.

Gilroy, Paul. (1987) *There Ain't No Black in the Union Jack.* Routledge.

Grant, A and Stringer K. (1995) *Uniting the Kingdom? The Making of British History.* London.

Griffith, P (ed) & Leonard, M (ed). (2002) *Reclaiming Britishness.* British Council.

Hasseler, S. (2000) *The Super-Rich: The Unjust New World of Global Capitalism.* Palgrave Macmillan.

Herman, Arthur. (2005) *To Rule the Waves: How the British Navy Shaped the Modern World.* Harper Perrenial.

Hobsbawm, E.J. (1992) *The Invention of tradition.* Cambridge University Press.

James, Lawrence. (1998) *The Rise and fall of the British Empire.* London, Abacus.

Kumar, Kristan. (2003) *The Making of English National Identity.* Cambridge.

Langlands, Rebecca. (1999) 'Britishness or Englishness? The historical problem of national identity in Britain' *Nations and Nationalism 5.*

MacKenzie John M. (1984) *Propaganda and Empire. The*

Manipulation of British Public Opinion, 1880-1960. Manchester University Press.

Mandler, Peter. (2006) *The English National Character: The History of an Idea from Edmund Burke to Tony Blair*. Yale University Press.

Michell, J.F. (1999) *Who Wrote Shakespeare?* Thames & Hudson.

Newman, Gerald. (1989) *The Rise of English Nationalism: A Cultural History 1740-1830*. London.

O'Farrell, J. (2008) *An Utterly Impartial History of Britain: (or 2000 Years of Upper Class Idiots in Charge)*. London, Black Swan.

Paxman, Jeremy. (1998) *The English: A Portrait of a People*. London.

Perryman, Mark. (2008) *Imagined Nation: England After Britain*. Lawrence & Wishart.

Preston, P.W. (2004) *Relocating England: Englishness in the new Europe*. Manchester.

Robbins, Keith. (1998) *Great Britain: Identities, Institutions and the Idea of Britishness*. Harlow.

Sampson, Anthony. (2004) *Who Runs This Place? The Anatomy of Britain in the 21st Century*.

Storey, Peter & Childs, Peter. (2007) *British Cultural Identities*. Routledge.

Taylor, D.J. (1993) *After the War*. Chatto and Windus.

Thomson, J.L. (2000) *Politicians, the Press and Propaganda: Lord Northcliffe and the Great War, 1914-19*. Kent state Press. USA.

Ward, P. (2004) *Britishness Since 1870*. Routledge, London.

Ware, V. (2007) *Who Cares about Britishness?* London, Arcadia Books.

Weight, Richard. (2002) *Patriots: National Identity in Britain 1940-2000.* London.

Wellings, Ben. (2002) 'Empire-nation: national and imperial discourses in England', *Nations and Nationalism 8.*

Williams, H. (2006) *Britain's Power Elites: The rebirth of the ruling class.* London, Constable and Robinson.

Wright, Patrick. (1985) *On Living in an old country.* Verso books

Up The British